Stuart Yarnold

Upgrading and Fixing a PC

Third Edition

In easy steps is an imprint of In Easy Steps Limited
Southfield Road · Southam
Warwickshire CV47 0FB · United Kingdom
www.ineasysteps.com

Third Edition

Notice of Liability
Every effort has been made to ensure that this book contains accurate
and current information. However, In Easy Steps Limited and the
author shall not be liable for any loss or damage suffered by readers
as a result of any information contained herein.

Trademarks
Microsoft® and Windows® are registered trademarks of Microsoft
Corporation. All other trademarks are acknowledged as belonging to
their respective companies.

In Easy Steps Limited supports The Forest Stewardship Council (FSC),
the leading international forest certification organisation. All our titles
that are printed on Greenpeace approved FSC certified paper carry the
FSC logo.

MIX
Paper from
responsible sources
FSC® C020837

Printed and bound in the United Kingdom

ISBN 978-1-84078-430-5

Contents

1 Before You Start

This chapter is an introduction to the subject of computer upgrading and fixing, and offers some general advice on issues you should consider before you start pulling your PC to pieces.

Hot tip

If you are capable of wielding a screwdriver, you are capable of upgrading any part in a computer.

Don't forget

Removing and installing parts is easy. Getting the right part is not quite so easy, and thus a major part of this book is devoted to making sure you get this right.

Introduction

Given the pace at which computer technology is advancing, upgrading parts as they become obsolete is the only realistic way of having a PC that's always capable of handling the latest software and hardware. Many people though, are wary of delving inside the system case for various reasons. These include: a) ignorance of what lies within, b) fear of invalidating warranties, and c) fear of damaging the PC. So they take the PC to a computer store and put up with the inconvenience and cost.

However, it is a fact that the physical act of replacing a computer part is very easy to do and is something that virtually anyone is capable of. This book provides you with all the information you need, plus illustrated guides on how to install every component in the PC.

This is actually the simple bit, though. Getting the right part for your purpose and making sure it is compatible with your existing setup is more difficult as it requires some knowledge about the part in question. For example, say you are upgrading the hard drive: there are different types of this device, plus they come with various interfaces, e.g. SATA, SCSI. These interfaces all have pros and cons, which make them suitable for some setups and less so for others. Which will be the right one for your PC? What type of drive should you go for?

To ensure you make the right choices, you will find detailed descriptions of all the computer's parts and relevant specifications. This information will enable you to make an informed decision and so avoid an upgrade that, at best, does not produce the desired result and, at worst, does not work at all.

There is also the issue of setting up of devices. With some, such as a sound card, this is straightforward but with others there is a lot more involved. For example, hard drives need to be partitioned and formatted before they can be used. Other parts require settings in the BIOS to be altered. Everything you need to know in these respects is explained.

Upgrades don't always go to plan and sometimes the new part won't work. If it's an essential system component, the PC itself might not work. To cover this, we provide a troubleshooting chapter that will help you to resolve most types of fault.

Is an Upgrade Necessary?

Before you decide to replace a component, make quite sure that it actually needs to be replaced. Some can appear to be malfunctioning when in reality the problem lies elsewhere, and others can be rejuvenated in various ways. The following are some typical examples:

- Hard drive performance can be seriously affected by a process known as fragmentation. So if you suspect that yours has a problem, you should always try defragmenting it first. These devices can also develop bad sectors, which can be the cause of data loss. Running the Windows disk repair utility will fix this

- When it comes to the speed of the PC, many people are fixated with the CPU – they think upgrading this part is guaranteed to give the system a boost. While it will to a certain extent, it is a fact that adding more memory will usually have a more significant impact

- Many devices have a chip that can be upgraded by a firmware update (known as flash upgrading). Most manufacturers provide firmware updates on their websites that reprogram these chips with a set of new instructions. Not only do the updates repair bugs, they often also add new features to the device in question. Check the manufacturers' websites to see if there are any worthwhile updates available for your devices before you replace them

- Optical drives have a focal lens inside them that is used to focus the laser beam with which they read data. This lens can become contaminated by airborne pollutants resulting in inability to read discs, and even crashes and freezing of the PC. Before you replace the drive, try using a lens cleaning kit

So unless you like spending money for the sake of it and making unnecessary work for yourself, see if there's a way to extend the life of existing parts before embarking on an upgrade.

Don't forget

Before buying a new hard drive for extra storage, try clearing your existing drive of redundant data. You may be surprised at how much space can be reclaimed by a good spring-clean.

Hot tip

Devices that can be improved by a flash upgrade include video cards, BIOS chips, printers and modems.

Buying Options

Having decided to buy a new part, the upgrader has two choices – retail or OEM. Both have their pros and cons.

Retail

A retail boxed CPU. The package includes the processor, heatsink/fan assembly, warranty and full instructions.

A retail product comes fully packaged in a printed box, and with a user manual, registration card and a full warranty. In many cases, bundled software will be included as well. You will also get everything needed to get the device into operation. For example, buy a CPU and a heatsink/fan assembly will be supplied as well.

Furthermore, retail products are more likely to be the genuine article – it is a fact that the computer parts market is flooded with counterfeit products of dubious origin (usually from the eastern hemisphere countries).

The disadvantage of buying retail products is that they cost more.

OEM

OEM is short for "Original Equipment Manufacturer". The term is used to describe a company that manufactures products to be sold under another company's brand name. These companies (typically, big computer manufacturers, such as Dell), buy large numbers of the various parts, put them together and then sell the finished computer under their own name.

OEM products also find their way on to the open market and can be bought from all the main outlets. The big advantage is that they are considerably cheaper than retail versions. However, there is a reason for this: they are sold in a plain box with no manual or bundled software, and usually with a limited warranty (typically, 30-60 days).

Also, very often, they will not be the complete article. For example, a retail hard drive will include the interface cables. OEM versions will not; you get the hard drive but nothing else.

So if you want to save money, buying OEM is the way to do it. Just remember that you will get no instructions, a limited warranty, and possibly an inferior product to boot. If you want guaranteed quality and all the "bells and whistles", pay the extra to get a retail product.

Sourcing Your Parts

Retail Outlets

Buying from a computer store is the quickest and safest method. If the part is faulty or you buy the wrong one by mistake, you can simply take it back and get a replacement.

Their main drawback is price. Stores have high overheads to pay and so charge high prices. Also, the staff in these places are often not too knowledgeable regarding the products they are selling. If you need good (and honest) advice, it may not be forthcoming.

The large chain-stores are the worst in these respects. Smaller, specialist computer stores are better and will usually offer good and impartial advice. Prices may not be any lower (they may even be higher) but the quality of service is usually far superior.

Mail Order

The beauty of mail order is that it enables buyers to compare prices without having to trudge around different stores. Also, sales staff are generally more clued-up than they are in stores.

The main advantage though, is that prices will be considerably less than in stores.

The Internet

Just about every product under the sun can be bought online these days and computer parts are no exception.

There are many websites that specialize in this area: two good examples of which are www.dabs.com in the UK and www.newegg.com in the USA (shown left).

Goods bought online will be cheaper than anywhere else. A further advantage is that online catalogs usually offer much more information, e.g. product specifications, than mail order catalogs.

Beware

A common scam in retail stores is selling OEM products at the full retail price. Don't fall for this; if the product isn't supplied in the manufacturer's box, don't buy it unless you can negotiate a substantial discount.

Beware

Internet retailers are not above a few scams of their own. So don't buy anything from a site that doesn't provide a contact telephone number. Emails can be ignored; persistent calls can't be.

Precautions

If you follow the instructions in this book, you should encounter no difficulties as a result of any upgrades that are made. If you don't, or inadvertently damage a component, you could have real problems.

One of these, potentially, is loss of data. While we're not saying that this is likely, it is a possibility. Therefore, you are strongly advised to make a backup of any data on the PC that you do not wish to lose before you get started.

To do it, you will need a backup medium (a DVD writer, a second hard drive or a USB flash drive), and possibly a backup program as well depending on the level of backup.

The simplest method is to go through the hard drive methodically and copy the required data to the backup medium. The problem with this way of doing it is that it is very easy to miss stuff. Unless you are an organized type of person, and thus know exactly where everything is, you may not back up everything you need to.

A safer way is to back it all up. In this case, you will need a backup program, such as the one supplied by Windows.

Hot tip

Don't forget to back up items such as Internet favorites, emails, etc.

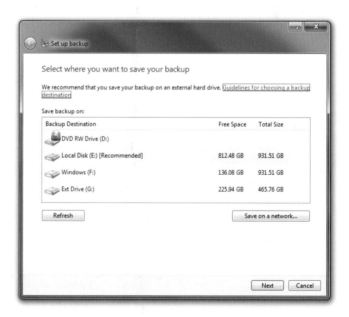

With this program (and others of its type), you can do a complete or selective backup.

2 Discovering Your PC

The most crucial aspect of upgrading is ensuring the new device is compatible with the rest of the system. We explain how to get detailed information on every part in the computer.

Inside the Computer

Power supply unit (PSU)

Motherboard

Memory (RAM)

Central processing unit and
heatsink/fan assembly

Expansion card

Expansion sockets

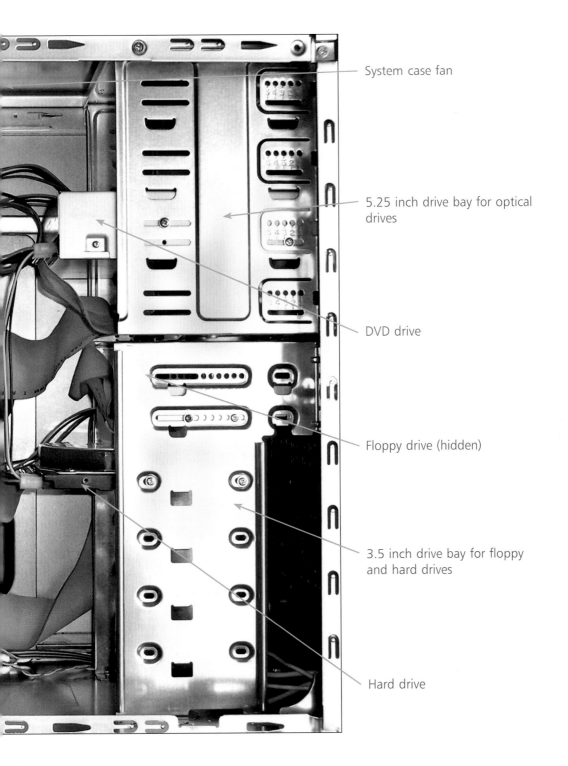

System case fan

5.25 inch drive bay for optical drives

DVD drive

Floppy drive (hidden)

3.5 inch drive bay for floppy and hard drives

Hard drive

Outside the Computer

Power supply unit on/off switch

PS/2 ports. The green one is for the mouse, the purple for the keyboard

VGA socket. Used to connect monitors to the PC

USB ports. USB is the standard type of connection

Video card VGA output to the monitor

Power supply unit fan air intake

Power cord socket

DVI socket. Used to connect LCD monitors

HDMI socket. Used to connect external video equipment

LAN (local area network) socket

eSATA socket. Used to connect external hard drives

Motherboard audio sockets.

Video card DVI output to the monitor

Sound card audio sockets

S/NO: 050467328

The Motherboard

Ports CPU power CPU socket Chipset Memory slots Motherboard power

BIOS chip

PCI Express x16 video card socket

PCI Express x1 socket

PCI socket

ATA drive socket

SATA drive sockets

Motherboard Sockets

Every component in a computer system is connected to the motherboard. To facilitate this, these boards provide sockets, or slots, of various types.

Video Card Sockets

Video cards use either the Advanced Graphics Port (AGP) interface (older cards) or the PCI-Express x16 interface (more recent cards). These are high-speed buses that boost the performance of these cards considerably.

PCI-Express x16 is a much faster interface than AGP and is the recommended option. AGP is, in fact, nearly obsolete now.

PCI and PCI-Express Sockets

PCI-Express is currently the standard interface for the connection of expansion cards to the system, and all modern motherboards provide at least two PCI-Express x1 sockets for this purpose.

Most motherboards also still provide one or two of the older PCI sockets that were superseded by PCI-Express. However, more recent motherboards may not so if you have a PCI card that you wish to keep using, check this out.

Hot tip

Note that PCI-Express x16 video card sockets are always a different color to the white PCI and PCI-Express sockets.

Hot tip

Unlike PCI, which uses a standard sized socket, the PCI-Express interface uses sockets of various sizes – x1, x2, x4, x8, x12 and x16. The larger the socket, the higher the speed at which data is transferred.

18

PCI Express x16 socket (for video cards)

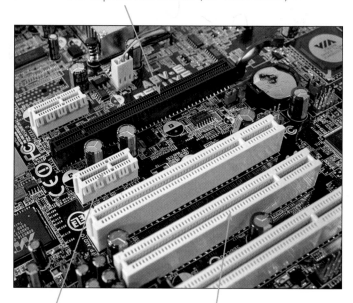

PCI Express x1 socket   PCI socket

Drive Sockets

The computer's internal drives (hard, floppy and optical) connect to the motherboard via either ATA or SATA interface sockets.

SATA 2 is the current standard and modern motherboards provide several of these sockets. More recent boards will also provide a couple of the faster SATA 3 sockets. Many boards still offer the older ATA interface as well for backward compatibility.

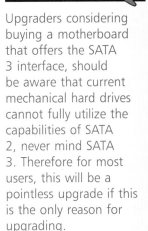

Hot tip

Upgraders considering buying a motherboard that offers the SATA 3 interface, should be aware that current mechanical hard drives cannot fully utilize the capabilities of SATA 2, never mind SATA 3. Therefore for most users, this will be a pointless upgrade if this is the only reason for upgrading.

However, this does not apply to the new SATA 3 solid state drives (SSDs). The data transfer speed of these devices would be throttled if used with SATA 2.

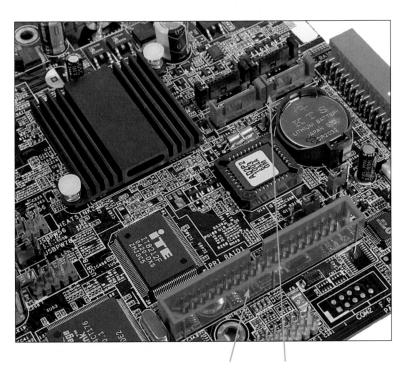

This motherboard provides both ATA and SATA connections

Ports

At the top-right of the motherboard are its input/output ports. These enable the user to connect peripheral devices to the system without having to open up the system case.

Most current motherboards provide all the ports shown on page 16.

CPU and Memory

The PC's processor (the CPU) and its memory (RAM) are both located on the motherboard and, with the BIOS chip, are the only of its components that can be upgraded.

CPU

The CPU plugs into the motherboard via a large square socket that is usually located towards the top-left of the board (in ATX motherboards, which most are). Mounted on top of the CPU is a heatsink/fan assembly, which keeps the device cool. In operation, therefore, the CPU is not visible.

CPU hidden by the heatsink/fan assembly

Heatsink/fan assembly removed revealing the CPU

Memory (RAM)

Computer memory consists of a number of semiconductor chips mounted on an oblong circuit board. These circuit boards, or RAM modules as they are known, plug into a socket on the motherboard, which is usually situated to the left of the CPU. Most motherboards provide several of these sockets.

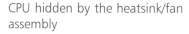

Memory module installed in one of two available sockets on the motherboard

Expansion Cards

Expansion cards do what their name suggests – they expand the capabilities of a computer. They connect to the motherboard via its PCI or PCI-Express sockets.

The most common of these are:

- Video cards
- Sound cards
- Wireless network cards

The easiest way of identifying them is by their input and output sockets.

Video cards have either a blue VGA socket or a white DVI socket, or both. They are unmistakable in any case due to their size and fans

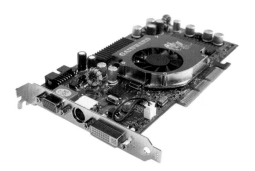

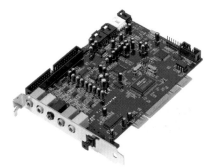

Sound cards have a number of colored sockets, usually blue, green, black and orange. The sockets are often stamped as Mic, Line in, Line out, etc

Wireless network cards are small circuit boards with a single socket for the connection of an aerial

Drive Units

All PCs have a hard drive and an optical (DVD, Blu-ray) drive. Older PCs will also probably have a floppy drive as well.

These devices are all located in the drive cages at the front of the system case, as shown below.

Optical Drive

Floppy Drive

Hard Drive

Full size and midi cases will have room for several drives of each type. Desktop cases will only have room for one hard drive and one optical drive.

System Details

When replacing or adding a new component to your PC, you need to know some relevant details. The following are some typical examples:

- You've decided to upgrade your video card to a PCI-Express model (or add one). However, before you do this, you need to know if your motherboard supports PCI-Express

- Your PC is running slowly and you suspect that more memory is needed. Before you go out and buy some though, you will need to find out how much you currently have, and also what type of memory it is

- You decide to flash upgrade your BIOS. For this operation to be successful, it is essential that you know the model numbers of both the BIOS chip and the motherboard

If you still have the manual that came with the PC, all the required information should be available from it. If you don't though, you need another source. Your first port of call will be Windows itself.

All versions of this operating system provide a system information utility (see margin note) called System Information. This will tell you many things about your PC, one of which is details of all its hardware devices.

Hot tip

Many manuals supplied by PC manufacturers can be somewhat non-specific. When looking for details of a certain part, you may find references to different models of that part used in various versions of the PC, which can be confusing. A good system information utility tells you exactly what's in the PC sitting on your desk and nothing else.

Hot tip

System Information gives you details of all the hardware and software installed in your system, Internet settings, and even devices that are faulty.

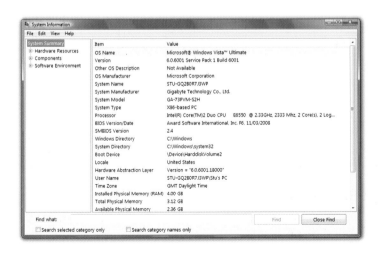

...cont'd

Don't forget

SiSoft Sandra is available at www.sisoftware.net. You will find several versions of this useful utility. The one that's free is the Lite version. Not all the modules are enabled with this but the ones you need are.

However, while System Information is undoubtedly useful, there are many third-party system information utilities that tell you a great deal more about your computer. One of these is SiSoft Sandra, a free version of which is available for download from the Internet (see margin note).

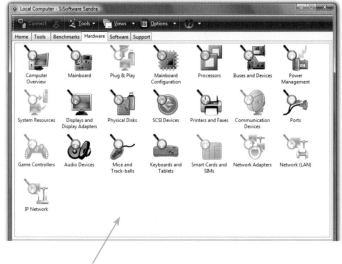

SiSoft Sandra consists of a number of modules, each of which relate to a specific part of the system

In this example we are looking at the motherboard module. As you can see from the size of the scrollbar, there is a tremendous amount of information available here

This utility is highly recommended and will give you all the information you need about your system.

3 A Faster PC

The components that most influence the speed at which a computer runs are the CPU and the memory. Both of them are available in a range of models, each with specifications and features that make them suitable for certain applications. In this chapter, we show how to make sure the parts you buy are correct for your purposes.

Is a CPU Upgrade Necessary?

The usual reason for upgrading a CPU is to make the PC faster, and most people expect to see a significant improvement by doing so. However, the extra performance gained may not be as much as they expect. For example, say, a 1.9 GHz CPU is replaced with a 3.8 GHz model; you may think that this will double the speed of the PC and that everything will happen twice as fast.

Unfortunately, it won't. While the PC will undoubtedly be more responsive, it won't bootup in half the time, programs will not open twice as quickly, etc. The extra processing capacity will become apparent only when an application that actually needs it is run. Whereas before, the PC may have struggled to cope, now it will run effortlessly.

So if your current CPU can handle your applications comfortably, upgrading it will make no significant difference to the performance of your PC (it would be like driving an Indy car in rush hour traffic – plenty of power but no way of using it).

However, should you develop an interest in CPU-intensive applications, such as video editing, PC gaming, desktop publishing, etc., a CPU upgrade will definitely pay dividends.

The CPU Market

Intel CPUs

Top of the Intel range are the Xeon and the Itanium, which are aimed at the server market. These are seriously high-performance processors and are priced accordingly. For the upgrader they do not really come into the equation.

Next up are the Core i7, Core i5 and Core i3 CPUs (in that order) with which Intel currently rule the Desktop PC market. Also available are older Core 2 Duo, Dual-Core Pentium and Celeron CPU's. We'll take a look at these in more detail.

Core i7 CPU

Intel's flagship product for Desktop PCs is the Core i7 range of processors. In the main, these CPUs feature four processors with Hyper-Threading technology, which creates an extra four *virtual* processors. They also come with Intel's Turbo Boost feature, which dynamically increases the CPU's speed beyond the base speed when an application requires a boost in processing power.

Beware

Do not be taken in by the marketing hype surrounding CPUs. It is a fact that most home systems run perfectly well with a low- to mid-range model.

Hot tip

Before replacing your CPU, try installing extra memory. In most cases, this will make a greater improvement to the PC's performance than a CPU upgrade will.

Another i7 feature is an integrated memory controller that enables three channels of DDR3 1600 MHz memory, and thus provides a considerable increase in processing efficiency.

i7 CPUs also have a new feature called the QuickPath Interconnect (QPI) system. This is a replacement for the old Front Side Bus (FSB) and provides a more efficient and faster data route between the processor and the motherboard.

In summary, i7's are high-performance CPUs and are intended for power users and gamers who require powerful systems.

Core i5 CPU

Next in Intel's Desktop range is the Core i5 CPU. As with all processor ranges, there are several different models of this CPU. Most of the i5s have two cores (instead of four as with the i7 range). Only the i5-750 and the i5-750S are quad-core CPUs.

However, the i5-750 and the i5-750S do not have Hyper-Threading technology unlike the two-core i5's. This enables the latter to also have two virtual cores, which to a degree mitigates the loss of performance due to having only two physical cores.

Also lacking is triple-channel memory support – i5s use traditional dual-channel memory configuration. Yet another drawback is the use of a scaled-down version of the QuickPath Interconnect (QPI) system used in the Core i7s, which is known as the Direct Media Interface (DMI). The Turbo Boost feature is available though.

To summarize, the main differences between the i7 and the i5 are:

- No Core i5 CPU has more than four physical or virtual cores as opposed to the i7s, which all have either eight (in four core models) or twelve (in six-core models). This means that i5s are not as fast under heavily multi-threaded workloads

- No triple-channel memory for the i5 results in an overall loss in system efficiency compared to the i7

- The Core i7 uses the QuickPath Interconnect (QPI) system, while the Core i5 makes do with the less efficient Direct Media Interface (DMI)

Hot tip

At the very top of the i7 range are several CPUs that feature no less than six cores.

Hot tip

Virtual cores do not provide the same level of processing power that physical cores do. However, they enable the operating system to schedule more threads or processes simultaneously, thus increasing the efficiency of the CPU.

...cont'd

- The Core i5 CPUs have a smaller Level 3 cache memory size, typically 4-6 MB as opposed to the 8 MB of the i7s

Core i3 CPU

The i3 is the baby of the Core i range of CPUs and thus comes with the lowest specifications. As with most of the i5s, these processors have two physical cores and Hyper-Threading technology to create two virtual cores.

Multi-channel memory support is restricted to dual-channel and they don't have the Turbo Boost feature. It is the latter that differentiates them from the i5s. Otherwise, they are similar.

The Core i3 is basically a highly specified budget CPU and provides excellent value for money.

Older Intel CPUs

Prior to the introduction of the Core i7, i5 and i3 ranges, the Core 2 Duo range were Intel's premier Desktop CPUs. These excellent processors are still available and are now very competitively priced. However, good as they are, even the Core i3 provides better overall system performance due to the new technologies built in to these CPUs.

Also still available are Pentium, and Celeron, dual-core CPUs which, as with the Core 2 Duo range, provide very good value for money.

AMD CPUs

At the time of writing, AMD CPUs are generally considered to be not as good as Intel's offerings.

Desktop processors are available in two main ranges: the Athlon II and the Phenom II. AMD also produce the highly specified Opteron, which is designed for the server market where it competes with Intel's Itanium and Xeon.

Phenom II

The Phenom II X6 is currently AMD's top of the range Desktop CPU and has six cores. It utilizes AMD's Turbo Core technology, which does exactly the same as Intel's Turbo Boost feature – i.e. providing a boost in processing power when it is needed.

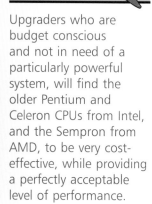

Hot tip

Upgraders who are budget conscious and not in need of a particularly powerful system, will find the older Pentium and Celeron CPUs from Intel, and the Sempron from AMD, to be very cost-effective, while providing a perfectly acceptable level of performance.

It also has Hyper-Transport Technology, which provides improved access times to system I/O for better performance.

Note that no AMD CPU currently supports triple-channel memory configuration. If this is something you require, the choice is clear – an Intel CPU. Also, AMD does not provide a technology similar to Intel's Hyper-Threading so, currently, an otherwise like-for-like AMD CPU will always be inferior to an Intel CPU equipped with Hyper-Threading.

The rest of the Phenom range consist mainly of four-core processors of various clock speeds and cache sizes.

Athlon II

Quite simply, the Athlon II CPU is a Phenom II CPU but without any Level 3 cache, and with lower clock speeds. Accordingly, it offers a lower performance level.

These CPUs are available in four-, three-, and two-core models.

Older AMD CPUs

The AMD Sempron CPU has been around a long time now but with a clock speed of 2.8 GHz, is still a capable performer. This CPU is available in both single- and dual-core models and so can be used even in a multi-tasking environment, assuming the applications being run are not too demanding.

Intel or AMD?

The architecture of Intel's Core i range is more up-to-date than that of AMD's Phenom range and provides new features, e.g. triple-channel memory support, that AMD haven't matched.

Accordingly, Intel CPUs currently offer superior performance.

However, it's not all roses in the Intel camp. On a cost/performance ratio, AMD CPUs do offer better value and, for this reason, are the preferred option for many people.

It also has to be said that while their processors are currently no match for those from Intel, they do provide perfectly adequate performance.

What CPU Do You Need?

All personal computers can be placed in one of four categories: low-end, mid-range, high-end, and gaming machines. The CPU you buy will, to a large degree, be dictated by which of these categories your PC is in, or intended to be in.

High-End Systems

These systems are predominantly servers and workstations, which require the most powerful (and most expensive) processors, i.e. Intel's Xeon and Itanium, and AMD's Opteron.

Upgraders requiring out-of-the-ordinary performance at a more affordable price, will be suitably served by a six- or four-core CPU such as those from Intel's Core i7 range. The only CPUs from AMD that belong in this category are the 6-core Phenom IIs.

Mid-Range Systems

Home computers are mostly in this class of computer and the range of suitable CPUs is vast. These PCs tend to be used for a range of applications, some of which need a reasonably powerful CPU, and others don't. For example, PC games that aren't too CPU-intensive, office applications, email, and the Internet.

All of these will run very nicely with any CPU from Intel's Core i5 range, a top-end model from the Core i3 range, a mid- to top-end model from the Core 2 Duo range, or a top-end dual-core Pentium.

Suitable AMD CPUs include any Phenom II CPU and mid- to top-end Athlon II CPUs.

Low-End Systems

Basic applications such as playing simple games like FreeCell, email, and web browsing require very little from the CPU. Suitable Intel processors include low-end CPUs from the Core 2 Duo range and dual-core Pentiums. Low-end Athlon IIs from AMD will also fit the bill.

Right at the bottom of the CPU market are Intel's Celeron and AMD's Sempron. These are both available in dual-core versions and offer surprisingly good performance. They are also extremely cheap. However, buying either will be investing in yesterday's technology and really doesn't make much sense as a few dollars more will get you a much more capable Athlon II or dual-core Pentium.

Gaming Machines

If you are upgrading your CPU with a view to PC gaming, you should be aware that to get the best out of today's 3D games in terms of frame rate (speed), and graphic and sound options, a seriously powerful CPU will be required.

Upgraders for whom nothing but the best will do will find that Intel's Core i7-990X Extreme 3.46 GHz CPU is currently the only choice. With the exception of CPUs designed for server use, such as the Xeon and Opteron, this is the most powerful (and expensive) CPU available. Featuring six cores, it provides a level of performance that gaming platforms such as Microsoft's Xbox, simply cannot match.

You should be also be aware that these high-end CPUs require the rest of the system to be of equal quality. This will probably mean that your motherboard has to be upgraded as well, not to mention replacing your memory with high-performance modules. You will also need a high-end video card.

However, if you are prepared to compromise on the quality of gameplay, perfectly acceptable performance can be had from any of the CPUs in Intel's Core i7 range, and AMD's Phenom II X6.

Hot tip

Online gaming is one of the most demanding applications for a PC and will require a highly specified machine.

CPU Specifications

Now that you have a general idea of what type of CPU is required in relation to your intended use of the PC, the next task is to choose a specific model. This means looking at the specifications. The following are the ones that should be considered:

Clock Speed

This is the speed at which a CPU runs and is measured as a frequency, e.g. 3.0 GHz (3000 million cycles per second). As every action (instruction) carried out by the CPU requires one or more cycles, it follows that the higher the clock speed, the more actions it will be able to carry out in any given period, i.e. the greater its processing capacity.

Be aware though, that there is a lot more to a CPU's performance than just clock speed. For example, you can buy a 3.0 GHz version of both the Celeron and the Pentium; the Celeron, however, is considerably slower and one of the reasons is that it has an FSB speed (see below) of 800 MHz, while the Pentium's is 1066 MHz. So although they both have the same processing power, the Pentium transfers data to the system more quickly as it has a faster FSB.

Front Side Bus (FSB)

A CPU's FSB is a communication channel through which data passes from the CPU to the system and vice versa. Because it is the main data channel in a PC, it is sometimes referred to as the system bus.

All CPUs have a clock speed that is considerably faster than their FSB, so the FSB speed is typically a ratio of the CPU's speed. For example, a Pentium CPU that runs at 2.4 GHz with an FSB speed of 400 MHz, will have a CPU/FSB ratio (known as the clock multiplier) of 6:1.

Without going into the reasons, the lower the ratio, the more efficiently the CPU will work. Therefore, faster FSBs lead to better system performance.

Note that CPUs from AMD do not have an FSB as such; they use a technology known as Hyper-Transport (see page 34). The same applies to Intel's Core i range – these CPUs have had the FSB replaced by new high speed buses, which are similar in function to AMD's Hyper-Transport.

Don't forget

A CPU's clock speed is an important indication of its quality but is by no means the only one. You must also consider its FSB speed, the amount of cache memory and any special technology employed.

Don't forget

If you intend to buy a CPU that uses the traditional FSB, it is important that the FSB of both the motherboard and the memory match that of the CPU as closely as possible. If the memory's FSB, for example, is much slower than that of either the CPU or the motherboard, a data bottleneck will be the result. This will adversely affect system performance.

Core i3s and Core i5s use the Direct Media Interface (DMI), while the more expensive Core i7s use a faster version known as the QuickPath Interconnect (QPI) system. As with any AMD CPU, if you buy any of these processors, CPU FSB speed will not be an issue.

However, older CPUs from Intel (Celerons, Pentiums and the Core 2 Duo range) do have an FSB.

Cache Memory

Cache memory is an area of high-speed memory built-in to the CPU, which is used to store frequently accessed data. Since this data doesn't have to be retrieved from the much slower system memory, overall performance is improved considerably. Going back to the Pentium/Celeron comparison on page 32, the Pentium typically, has twice as much cache memory as does the Celeron.

Traditionally, CPUs have commonly used two types of cache – level 1 (L1) and level 2 (L2). L2 is slightly slower than L1 but is larger, and is the one usually specified by vendors. However, modern multi-core CPUs also have a third cache, level 3.

Other factors to consider, include:

Cooling – CPUs generate a lot of heat and so must be adequately cooled by a suitable heatsink/fan assembly to prevent them from burning out. If you buy a retail CPU, this won't be a problem – an approved unit will be included. However, if you buy an OEM CPU, you will have to buy one separately. The important thing here is to make sure that the heatsink/fan assembly you buy is recommended for use with the CPU. If it is not, you could well have heat related problems down the line.

Power – this will be a consideration only if you are buying one of the latest high-end CPUs. These devices draw a lot of power, so you must make sure that the power supply unit (PSU) is up to the job (see page 130).

Technology – Intel and AMD both employ various technologies, such as Hyper-Transport and Hyper-Threading on certain of their processors. These make a considerable difference to both the performance and the price of the CPUs in question. We'll look at these technologies next.

Hot tip

One of the main factors in the price of CPUs is the amount of cache memory. This type of memory is extremely expensive and is the reason that two CPUs of otherwise similar specifications can have a big price differential.

CPU Technologies

Hyper-Transport

Hyper-Transport technology is unique to AMD CPUs, and is basically a high-speed, low-power communication channel (bus) that enables the CPU to communicate with the system at high speed and thus with greater data throughput. Effectively, it's a souped-up FSB.

CPUs that employ it have two data channels – one to communicate with memory and one (the Hyper-Transport bus) to communicate with the motherboard chipset. Thus, these CPUs can communicate with both the memory and the chipset simultaneously – CPUs without Hyper-Transport cannot do this as they have only one communication channel.

Another advantage of the Hyper-Transport bus is that it provides a route for the transmission of data and a separate route for its reception. In the traditional architecture used by other processors, a single route is used both for the transmission and for the reception of data.

Note that all modern AMD CPUs are equipped with this technology.

Hyper-Threading

Not to be confused with AMD's Hyper-Transport, Hyper-Threading is an Intel technology that offers improved multi-tasking performance by creating a virtual CPU that appears to the operating system as another, physical, CPU. This facilitates the handling of two simultaneous processes.

Intel claims up to a 30 per cent speed improvement in comparison to an otherwise identical CPU. The performance gain achieved is very application dependent, however, and some programs actually slow down slightly when used with a Hyper-Thread CPU.

Is it worth having? If you do serious multi-tasking, the answer is yes. Otherwise, no.

Note that for Hyper-Threading to function properly, it must be supported not only by the motherboard, but also by the application being run.

In essence, it is a poor man's multi-core CPU – cheaper but not as effective.

Don't forget

If you want a Hyper-Threaded system, you will need more than a Hyper-Thread CPU. For this technology to work, it is necessary to have a Hyper-Thread compatible motherboard, and also software.

Multi-Core

Multi-core Desktop CPUs employ two, four or six processor cores on the same chip. Each core functions and processes data independently and is coordinated by the operating system.

With regard to the actual speed of the CPU, multi-cores do not have the impact one may think. For example, a two-core CPU will not be twice as fast as a single-core CPU; it will in fact be about 50 % faster, and a quad-core will be about 25 % faster than a two-core.

The main advantage offered by multi-core CPUs is much improved multi-tasking and, to a lesser extent, increased performance for multi-thread applications.

A commonly asked question these days is "How many core's do I need?" The simple answer is that for most users a single-core CPU is perfectly adequate. However, given that these are rapidly disappearing from the market, for general PC use a two-core CPU is recommended.

It's only gamers, and power users who run CPU-intensive applications or many applications simultaneously, who will see any benefit from four- or six-core CPUs.

Turbo Boost

Found only on higher-end Intel CPUs, Turbo Boost is a technology that enables dynamically increasing CPU clock speed on demand. Turbo Boost activates when the operating system requests the highest performance state of the processor.

Assuming the processor has not reached its thermal and electrical limits, when the user's workload requires additional performance, the processor clock speed will dynamically increase in increments of 133 MHz until either a thermal or power limit, or the maximum speed for the number of active cores, is reached. Conversely, when any of the limits are exceeded, the processor frequency will automatically decrease in decrements of 133 MHz until the processor is again operating within its limits.

AMD have a similar technology on its high-end Phenom CPUs known as Turbo Core.

Beware

Don't confuse dual-core with dual-processor. A dual-processor system has two separate CPUs, each of which has its own hardware. Thus, it provides much better performance than a dual-core CPU, which has to share associated hardware, such as the memory controller and front side bus.

64-Bit Architecture

All modern CPUs support 64-bit architecture. But what is it and how does it benefit the user?

The term "64-bit" when referring to a CPU means that in one integer register the CPU can store 64 bits of data. Older CPUs, which could only support 32-bit architecture, could store only 32 bits of data in a register, i.e. half the amount. Therefore, 64-bit architecture provides better overall system performance as it can handle twice as much data in one clock cycle.

However, the main advantage provided by 64-bit architecture is the huge amount of memory it can support. CPUs operating on a 32-bit Windows Vista or Windows 7 system can utilize a maximum of 3 GB, whereas on a 64-bit system they can utilize up to 192 GB.

The caveat is that a 64-bit system requires all the software to be 64-bit compatible, i.e. it must be 64-bit software. This includes the operating system and device drivers (this is why more recent versions of Windows [XP, Vista and 7] are supplied in both 32-bit [x86] and 64-bit [x64] versions). Note that most 32-bit software will run on a 64-bit system but the advantages provided by 64-bit architecture won't be available.

So who will benefit from a 64-bit system and who won't? The simple answer is that every PC user will benefit as their system will be more efficient. Don't expect to see major speed gains over a 32-bit system when running day-to-day applications such as web browsers, word processing and 2D games, though; you probably won't notice any.

However, when running CPU-intensive applications that require large amounts of data to be handled, e.g. video editing, 3D games, CAD, etc, 64-bit systems will be considerably faster. Also, if you need more memory than the current limit of 3 GB possible with a 32-bit system, 64-bit architecture allows you to install as much as you want (up to the limitations of the motherboard).

So to get a 64-bit system, all you have to do is buy a modern CPU and install a 64-bit version of your chosen operating system. Don't forget that all your software and device drivers will also have to be 64-bit versions.

Installing a CPU

Ideally, the motherboard will have been removed from the system case; not only does this make the procedure considerably easier but there is also less chance of damaging the motherboard.

That said, it is quite possible to do the job in situ as long as you exercise some care. However, with anything other than a mid- or full-tower system case (both of which give unrestricted access), you will probably have to first remove the power supply unit, as this device will impede access. You may also have to disconnect the CD/DVD, floppy, and hard drive interface cables.

1 If you are replacing an existing CPU, you may find that it is welded to the heatsink by thermal paste, in which case you will have to separate them by inserting a thin blade and prising them apart

2 Having removed the heatsink/fan assembly, lift the socket locking lever and then move the load plate to gain access to the CPU socket, as shown below

Socket locking lever   Load plate

Hot tip

The procedure for installing CPUs is exactly the same for both Intel and AMD CPUs.

Beware

Beware of your body's electrostatic electricity when handling CPUs. Purchasing and using an electrostatic wriststrap is recommended.

...cont'd

Hot tip

Different CPUs use different methods of ensuring the CPU is inserted the correct way. The CPU in our example is notched on two sides and these engage in lugs on the socket.

3 Align the notches in the CPU with the corresponding lugs on the socket

4 Drop the CPU into the socket

5 Replace the load plate and then close the locking lever

Hot tip

Make sure the CPU is fitted correctly (all four sides must be flush with the socket) before you close the locking lever. Otherwise, you will bend and possibly break some of the pins.

Fitting a Heatsink and Fan

The next step is to fit the heatsink/fan assembly. The heatsink part of the assembly sits directly on top of the CPU and keeps it cool when the PC is running. To increase the efficiency with which it does this, a layer of thermal compound is placed between it and the CPU.

It is extremely important that this compound is in place as, without it, the CPU is quite likely to overheat. Many heatsinks come with thermal compound already applied as shown on the left. However, there are many that don't, in which case you will have to do it yourself; as you will if you are reusing an old heatsink.

It doesn't matter if the compound is applied to the top of the CPU or the bottom of the heatsink. Whichever way you choose, the trick is to get a very thin, even layer that covers the entire surface.

Hot tip

New heatsinks are supplied with a thermal pad in situ, as shown below. Be careful to keep your fingers off it as dead skin and oil reduces its effectiveness.

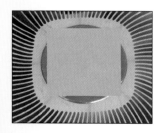

40

Squeeze a small blob of thermal compound on to the top of the CPU (or bottom of the heatsink)

Don't forget
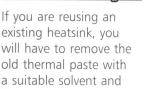

If you are reusing an existing heatsink, you will have to remove the old thermal paste with a suitable solvent and then replace it with new paste. This is available from any computer store in the form of either pads or a tube.

Using a piece of card, spread the compound evenly across the contact area. It should be as thin as you can get it

Now you can fit the heatsink. There are various methods of securing it in place, the most common one being a simple push-fit into pre-drilled holes in the motherboard. This is demonstrated in the example below:

1 Position the heat sink/fan assembly over the CPU and line up the four pins on the assembly with the corresponding holes in the motherboard

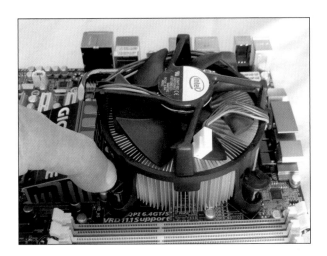

2 Push down on each pin in turn until it clicks into place. Finally, connect the CPU's fan to the motherboard's fan power supply

Don't forget

The final step is to connect the CPU fan to the motherboard's fan power supply (this will be a small 3-pin connector located near the CPU socket).

When is a Memory Upgrade Necessary?

When you buy a PC, it should come with an adequate amount of memory to run the operating system and software installed on it. Most will but in today's tough economic climate, some PC manufacturers' are cutting costs to the bone by shipping PCs with the bare minimum of memory required to run the operating system and non-demanding applications such as the Internet, word processing, etc.

While these PCs will work, using them may well be a somewhat frustrating experience. You could, of course, send the PC back but it will much be quicker, and probably cheaper as well, to install an extra memory module yourself.

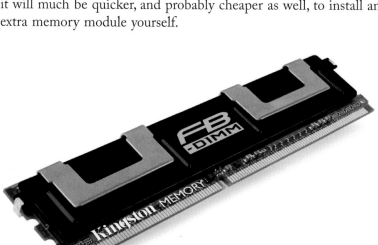

Even if the PC is ok to begin with though, because the memory requirements of both software and hardware increase with every succeeding version and model, the time will inevitably come when it no longer has enough.

This will be when your PC slows to an unacceptable level when running an application (or a number of applications simultaneously).

While installing a memory module is very simple to do, it is essential to make sure that the module you buy is compatible with your system. The following pages tell you everything you need to know to make sure you make the correct choice.

Hot tip

A very good indicator of lack of memory is a hard drive activity LED that is flashing constantly. When the system runs out of memory, it creates a memory file (known as virtual memory) on the hard drive, which it uses to keep things running.

Types of Memory

Double Data Rate SDRAM

The memory technology currently in vogue is Double Data Rate Synchronous Dynamic RAM, otherwise known as DDR. The vast majority of Desktop PCs are now using this type of memory as it's cheap, fast and reliable.

DDR memory is currently available in three versions: DDR1 (or just DDR), DDR2 and DDR3, and to enable you to determine which is best for your requirements you need to have some basic knowledge about it.

As with the CPU, memory transfers a given amount of data on every clock cycle. Before DDR came along, PC memory used Single Data Rate (SDR) technology that only employed the up side of a cycle. DDR, on the other hand, uses the down side as well, thus is able to transfer twice as much data in a clock cycle.

The first version of DDR, DDR1, has now been superseded by DDR2, which is currently the mainstream type of PC memory. The technology behind DDR2 is basically the same as with DDR1; the difference lies in the fact that in DDR2 modules the memory cells are clocked at 1/4 (rather than 1/2 as with DDR1) the rate of the bus. As a result, DDR2 operates at twice the speed of DDR1.

However, the writing is already on the wall for DDR2 as DDR3 is now on the market. The difference here is that DDR3 modules are clocked at 1/8 the rate of the bus, thus they operate at twice the speed of DDR2

As a result, DDR3 offers the same advantages over DDR2 as DDR2 does over DDR1. It's faster, it requires less power (1.5v), and it enables triple-channel memory configurations to improve even further the efficiency of the memory.

Another difference between the three types of DDR is the form factor. DDR1 has a 184-pin edge connector, DDR2 has a 240-pin edge connector and, while DDR3 also has a 240-pin edge connector, its socket locating key is in a different position.

Because of the difference in form factors, they are incompatible with each other, i.e. a motherboard designed for DDR2 will only be able to accept DDR2 modules.

Beware

Don't forget to check that the memory you buy is physically compatible with the motherboard.

cont'd

The first table shows the DDR1 modules currently available:

Version	Clock Speed	FSB Speed	Data Transfer Rate
PC1600	100 MHz	200 MHz	1.6 GBs
PC2100	133 MHz	266 MHz	2.1 GBs
PC2400	150 MHz	300 MHz	2.4 GBs
PC2700	166 MHz	333 MHz	2.7 GBs

The second table shows the range of DDR2 modules on the market and, from it, you can clearly see that it carries on where DDR1 left off. The slowest DDR2 module, PC2-3200, is faster, and has a higher data transfer rate, than the fastest DDR1 module, PC-2700.

Version	Clock Speed	FSB Speed	Data Transfer Rate
PC3200	200 MHz	400 MHz	3.2 GBs
PC4200	266 MHz	533 MHz	4.3 GBs
PC5300	333 MHz	667 MHz	5.4 GBs
PC6400	400 MHz	800 MHz	6.4 GBs
PC8500	533 MHz	1066 MHz	8.5 GBs

The third table shows what is available in the DDR3 line and, once again, we can see that DDR3 carries on where DDR2 left off.

Version	Clock Speed	FSB Speed	Data Transfer Rate
PC3-8500	533 MHz	1066 MHz	8.5 GBs
PC3-10600	667 MHz	1333 MHz	10.6 GBs
PC3-12800	800 MHz	1600 MHz	12.8 GBs
PC3-14900	933 MHz	1866 MHz	14.9 GBs
PC3-17000	1066 MHz	2133 MHz	17.0 GBs

On the next page, we look at some variations of DDR memory that are often the cause of confusion to buyers.

Error Checking Modules

When investigating the memory market, you will also come across other, apparently different, types of memory such as Parity, ECC, etc. We'll take a brief look at these.

- Parity – parity modules have an extra (parity) chip for error detection. This checks that data is correctly read or written by the memory module by adding additional bits and using a special algorithm. However, it will not correct any errors it may find

- ECC – ECC modules are very similar to parity modules. However, unlike parity modules, the ECC module will, in most cases, correct any errors it finds, depending on the type of error

- Buffered – buffered modules contain a buffer chip to help the module cope with the large electrical load required for large amounts of memory. The buffer electrically isolates the memory from the controller to minimize the load on the chipset

- Registered – very similar to buffered memory, these modules contain registers that hold the data for one clock cycle before it is moved on to the motherboard

All of the above modules are based on SDRAM technology and are available in DDR1, DDR2 and DDR3 versions. The difference between them and standard SDRAM memory is the fact that they incorporate some type of error-checking technique that increases their reliability (and hence that of the PC) considerably.

For this reason they are found predominantly in Servers and mission-critical systems. The typical home PC has no need for these types of memory.

The drawbacks of error checking memory is that it is considerably more expensive and also slower in operation due to the error-checking procedure.

Buying Memory

We've already seen what types of memory are available. Now we'll take a more specific look, and also consider other factors which will influence your decision.

Type of Memory

This is the first thing to decide and is a straightforward decision: DDR2 or DDR3 (although we have taken a brief look at it, DDR1 is now, in fact, obsolete).

Just because it is slower than DDR3 doesn't mean that DDR2 is a slouch; far from it, in fact. For the vast majority of users, it provides a performance level that is more than adequate. It is only when considering factors such as "future proofing" and triple-channel memory configurations, and in cases where a high-performance system is required, that DDR3 memory will be necessary.

You should also be aware that high-end DDR2 modules, e.g. PC2-8500, actually provide better performance than low-end DDR3 modules, e.g. PC3-8500 and PC3-10600. This is due to the higher latencies found in DDR3 memory (see page 48 for more on this). However, even with the high latencies, the high-end DDR3 modules, e.g. PC3-14900 and PC3-17000 are faster than DDR2 because of their higher clock cycles, which more than compensate for the latency issue.

Another factor to consider with regard to DDR3 is that motherboards that support this type of memory are considerably more expensive, so affordability may be a problem.

To summarize then, for most purposes DDR2 is perfectly adequate and, as already mentioned, high-end DDR2 is actually faster than low-end DDR3. However, assuming the higher cost of a DDR3 capable motherboard is not an issue, DDR3 memory is the recommended option, if only because it's the latest technology. This applies particularly if you are building a high-performance system.

Note that whichever version of DDR you go for, the module's specifications need to be in line with the rest of the system. Therefore, you also need to consider the following factors:

Don't forget

For typical computer uses, you need look no further than DDR2 SDRAM. Performance enthusiasts will consider high-performance modules such as Kingston's Hyper-X. Cutting-edge enthusiasts will be interested in DDR3 memory.

Don't forget

The real advantage of the huge bandwidths provided by DDR3 memory is only fully utilized in high-performance server systems. Home PCs simply don't need it.

Memory Specifications

Memory FSB

For the best possible system performance, ideally the memory's FSB speed will be equal to the CPU's, otherwise it becomes a performance bottleneck. The slower it is in relation to the CPU's the slower the system will be.

However, modern CPUs have high FSBs, typically 1333 MHz and higher, and the fastest mainstream DDR2 memory, PC2-8500, has an FSB of only 1066 MHz. So what are your options? There are three:

- Buy PC3-10600, and above, DDR3 modules. These do have CPU comparable FSBs. They are, however, expensive (as are motherboards designed to use DDR3)

- Use triple-channel memory. This increases the memory's data transfer rate and results in an effective memory speed increase of about 10-15 per cent

- Settle for a trade-off in terms of cost versus performance

The memory's FSB also needs to be supported by the motherboard. The easiest way to ensure you get this right is to look at the motherboard's specifications, which you will find at the relevant manufacturer's website. An example is shown below:

The specs show you the type, speed, and amount of memory supported by the board.

Beware

If you install a memory module rated at a speed higher than the motherboard and CPU are designed to handle, the memory will still work but only at the motherboard's maximum speed – you won't be getting the best out of it.

If you install a module rated at a speed lower than the motherboard or CPU FSB, this will create a data bottleneck in the system as the memory will not be able to keep up. The result will be degraded system performance.

Don't forget

To work in dual- or triple-channel mode, the modules must be identical (many memory manufacturers sell dual- and triple-channel kits for this purpose). Multi-channel must also be supported by both the motherboard and CPU.

cont'd

Don't forget

The online memory configurators found at the websites of major memory companies are a very useful way of determining exactly what type of memory will be compatible with your system.

Latency

A key performance indicator for memory modules is latency and the term refers to the length of time it takes a module to begin transferring the requested data. This metric is measured in clock cycles and there are many factors involved such as tRAS, tRP, tRCD and command rate. However the most important factor is known as CAS (Column Access Strobe).

DDR1 has CAS latencies of 2, 2.5 and 3, DDR2 has CAS latencies between 3 and 7, and DDR3 has CAS latencies between 6 and 10. Fairly obviously, the lower the CAS latency, the better. Remember however, that these figures are relative: DDR2 has higher latencies than DDR1 and DDR3 has higher latencies than DDR2, but compensate by having faster clock cycles.

Upgraders who want the best bang for their buck will definitely need to check this issue before parting with the cash.

Dual- and Triple-Channel Memory

Most current motherboards can run the system's memory in either dual- or triple-channel mode. Motherboards designed for DDR2 will run it in dual-channel mode and motherboards designed for DDR3 will run it in either dual- or triple-channel mode.

Mult-channel mode is basically a method of increasing the memory's bandwidth, which enables the system to run faster and more efficiently. For it to work, the installed modules must all be exactly the same. Note that the memory manufacturers sell dual- and triple-channel kits for precisely this purpose.

However, in most cases, the effective gains made over single-channel memory are usually modest – in the region of 10-15 per cent. It's only in systems that shift serious amounts of data, e.g. servers and work stations, that the full benefits will be seen.

Memory Capacity

The amount of memory that you need in your system is determined by the applications that you intend to run. Don't forget that this also includes the operating system.

The table on the next page provides an approximate guide to the amount of memory required for typical uses of a PC.

Hot tip

Instead of buying, say, two 512 MB modules, buy one 1 GB module. Not only will this be cheaper, it will leave you with spare slots for future memory upgrades.

Operating System	Low-Usage	Mid-Usage	High-Usage
Windows 7	1 GB	2 GB	4 GB
Windows Vista	512 MB	1 GB	2 GB
Windows XP	256 MB	512 MB	1 GB
Mac OS X	1 GB	1.5 GB	2 GB
Linux	512 MB	768 MB	1.5 GB

Low-usage is defined as resource-light applications, such as word-processing, web browsing, email, 2D games, data-entry, etc. If you tend to run several of these applications simultaneously, you should install the amount specified in the mid-usage column.

Mid-usage is running programs such as photo-editing, web applications, multimedia, sound-editing, printing, scanning, etc. If you run several of these at the same time, install the amount specified in the high-usage column.

High-usage is defined as 3D gaming (particularly online gaming), real-time video-editing, computer aided design (CAD), animation, 3D modeling, high-end desktop publishing, etc.

Note that 64-bit versions of Windows 7, Windows Vista and Windows XP will need twice the amount of memory specified above. Also, the figures are the minimum amount required.

Memory Manufacturers

Unlike the CPU, where the choice is essentially between Intel and AMD, both of whose products are high quality, there is any number of memory manufacturers.

As the memory plays a crucial role in the performance and reliability of a computer system, you must buy the best you can afford – this is not a component on which to economize.

Three manufacturers spring to mind here – Crucial, Corsair, and Kingston Technologies. Buy your memory from any of these companies and you won't go wrong.

Avoid cheap unbranded memory as you would the plague. Poor quality modules cause system crashes and lock-ups, which can be the cause of data loss.

Hot tip

Another consideration is your future memory requirements. Each succeeding version of Windows, and virtually all major software titles, require more memory than preceding versions did. For this reason, it makes sense to add a bit more to your system than you currently need.

49

Don't forget

For guaranteed quality, buy branded memory from well known manufacturers such as Kingston and Crucial.

Installing Memory Modules

Before you do anything, read the following paragraph:

The electrostatic electricity present in your body is absolutely lethal to memory chips. If you don't ground yourself to discharge it, just one touch can destroy the module.

So, if you have an electrostatic wrist strap now is the time to use it. Alternatively, touch the bare metal of the system case chassis or wear a pair of close fitting rubber gloves. We also recommend that you avoid standing on a carpet – this is the best way to build up a static charge.

When you do pick up the chip, hold it by the edges as far as possible, as shown below:

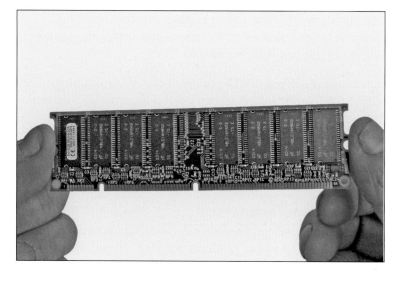

Another way to safeguard against electrostatic electricity is to buy a module that comes with a heat-spreader, as shown in the example below. This ensures that you cannot touch the circuitry inside.

Beware

Memory modules are the component most likely to be damaged by incorrect handling. Just one careless touch is all it takes, so be warned.

Don't forget

Memory modules are also available with a heat-spreader. While these are intended primarily as a means of dissipating heat, they also provide the added benefit of protection.

1 The first thing to do is open the retaining clips on each side of the slot/s you are going to use

Hot tip

If you are fitting modules in a dual- or triple-channel configuration, refer to the motherboard's manual for which sockets to use.

2 Align the cut-out on the module's edge connector with the engaging lug on the slot

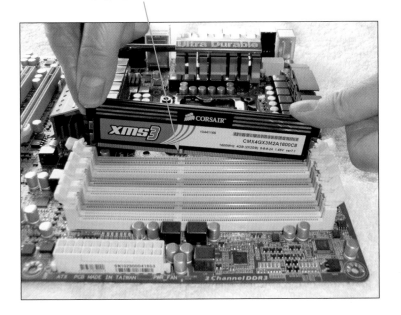

Beware

If you find yourself trying to force the module retaining clips to close, stop immediately. Either the module is not fully inserted or you are using the wrong type. In this situation, all you are likely to do is break the clips or damage the motherboard.

3 Press down on both ends. You will need to exert some firm pressure here

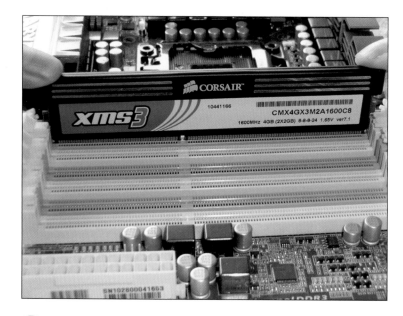

4 When the module is correctly seated, the retaining clips will close automatically

4 A More Versatile PC

To make a PC more versatile it is necessary to add to its existing capabilities. As these are inherent to the motherboard, doing so often requires that this device be upgraded as well. There are many factors that will influence this decision and this chapter ensures that you will make the correct one.

Is an Upgrade Necessary?

There are three reasons to upgrade a motherboard:

1) The existing one has failed

2) You want a more powerful PC

3) To modernize your system

However, this is not the easiest of tasks as it can mean literally stripping the system down to gain access to the board, and then rebuilding it. Also, because so many other parts are involved, the potential for something going wrong as a result is higher than with any other type of upgrade.

These are two good reasons to not do it unless absolutely necessary. Another is that a motherboard upgrade may require other components to be upgraded as well.

The older your system, the more likely this is. Components in vintage PCs (ten years, or more, old), will be incompatible with modern motherboards in virtually every respect. Even the case may need replacing. In this situation, a brand new PC makes more sense than a motherboard upgrade.

With systems between five and ten years old, the CPU and memory will almost certainly have to be replaced. It is also quite likely that some expansion cards, such as sound cards, will be using the old, and now virtually obsolete, PCI interface. Video cards will probably be AGP models, and thus will also be incompatible with modern motherboards.

A motherboard upgrade to accommodate a modern CPU could mean a new power supply unit as well. This is due to the high power requirements of these devices. It would be absolute folly to run one of the latest and greatest CPUs on an old 300 watt PSU; it would probably blow immediately, taking your new CPU with it.

The bottom line then, is that before you do it be sure that there is no alternative. Clearly, if the existing board has failed, it's a no-brainer. If it's a faster PC you want, try a memory upgrade first. If you need support for new technology, check that it can't be added to the existing motherboard in the form of a PCI or PCI-Express expansion card.

Buying a Motherboard

Because the motherboard is the central component in the PC, replacing it with a different model can, and often does, have ramifications with regard to other components in the PC.

Compatibility Issues

All PC hardware needs to be compatible with the motherboard, both in terms of technology, and method of connection. The most important are the CPU and memory.

CPU

The first consideration with the CPU is physical compatibility with the motherboard. This means that the board must have the socket that the CPU was designed to use. A quick look at the specifications will ensure you get this right. The CPU specs will specify the socket required, e.g. socket AM3, LGA775, LGA1156, etc. The motherboard specs will specify the socket provided.

The next consideration is the motherboard's FSB speed in relation to that of the CPU – these should be as closely matched as possible. For maximum performance, they will be the same. However, this is not a critical issue – the system will work whatever the disparity, but at the lower of the two speeds. Again, you need to look at the specifications.

Alternatively, use the system building guides provided by AMD (www.amd.com) and Intel (www.intel.com) on their websites. Just select the CPU you want and you will be presented with a list of compatible motherboards – it couldn't be easier.

Memory

There are three things you need to consider with relation to motherboards and memory.

1)   Can the board fully utilize the amount of memory installed?

2)   Does the board support the rated speed of the memory?

3)   Will the memory modules physically fit on the board?

With regard to the amount of memory, even low-end motherboards will be able to support 4 GB, while most will support 16, and a few 24 GB. As few people are going to need any more than 4 GB, in most cases it should not be an issue.

Hot tip

Many computer retail outlets supply kits, which comprise a matched motherboard, CPU and memory. This is an option for those who don't want the bother of matching the parts themselves.

Hot tip

Current 32-bit systems can use a maximum of 3.5 GB of memory. 64-bit systems can use well over 100 GB. In practice though, because motherboards currently offer a maximum of six DIMM slots, and the maximum size of a DIMM module is currently 4 GB, the maximum you can install on these boards is 24 GB.

However, as most home systems need no more than 2 GB of memory, 24 GB is still an enormous amount.

...cont'd

As far as speed is concerned, ideally the memory's FSB will be equal to the motherboard's FSB. It is not critical though, if it isn't.

For example, if you put a stick of high-speed PC2-8500 DDR2 memory, which runs at 1066 MHz into a motherboard that only supports 800 MHz, the system will still work. However, the memory will operate at the lower speed so you will not be getting the best out of it.

Unless you are reusing an old motherboard or memory module, you will have no problems fitting your memory into the board. Most memory modules in current use are DDR2 240-pin DIMMs, and the majority of mainstream motherboards will accept these. If you are using 240-pin DDR3 modules, you will need a motherboard that provides DDR3 sockets.

Form Factors

A motherboard's form factor relates to its physical dimensions and needs to be matched to the form factor of the system case and the power supply unit. This ensures that they are all physically compatible with each other, i.e. they fit in the case and the screw holes line up.

The vast majority of PCs these days use the ATX form factor, which is available in three sizes – ATX, Mini ATX and Micro ATX. ATX motherboards are used in full- and mid-tower system cases, Mini ATX in mini system cases, while Micro ATX boards are used in Desktop system cases.

If your system is housed in a full- or mid-tower case, you can use a motherboard built to any variation of ATX, as these cases are downward compatible, i.e. they have mounting points for all of them. If you have a Desktop case, however, you will be restricted to a Micro ATX board.

Making sure you get the correct size of motherboard for your case is straightforward as they are all advertised with the form factor used. For example: ABIT KV7 Via Socket AM3 Micro ATX. This tells you the motherboard manufacturer (Abit), the motherboard's model number (KV7), the chipset manufacturer (Via), the CPU socket type (Socket AM3) and the form factor (Micro ATX).

Motherboard Sockets

The motherboard's sockets allow you to expand and update your system as and when required.

PCI

For many years PCI was the standard interface for internal hardware devices. However, it has now been largely superseded by the PCI-Express interface. That said, there are still many expansion cards on the market that use PCI, e.g. sound cards and, for this reason, virtually all current motherboards provide one or two PCI sockets.

PCI-Express

This is an enhanced version of the PCI interface that provides much better performance and it will eventually replace the PCI interface. All motherboards provide several of these sockets so if you intend to fit any PCI-Express expansion cards all you need do is check that your chosen motherboard provides enough of them.

AGP

Used for video cards, the AGP interface, as with the PCI interface, has now been superseded by the PCI-Express x16 interface. Few modern motherboards provide this socket so if you have an AGP video card that you wish to reuse, you will probably have to hunt about for a board that supports it.

PCI-Express x16

This interface is currently the standard interface for video cards and provides much improved performance over the old AGP interface. It currently comes in two versions: PCI-Express x16, and the newer, and faster, PCI-Express 2.1 x16.

Drive

The current interface for connecting drive units to the system is SATA, which has superseded the ATA interface and provides many improvements. All modern motherboards provide several SATA sockets. As with PCI-Express, there are several versions, each providing improvements over the previous ones. The latest is SATA 3.0.

Most current motherboards also still provide the older ATA drive interface for backward compatibility.

Hot tip

Even if you currently have no PCI-Express devices or a SATA 3 drive, by buying a motherboard equipped with these technologies, your system will be future-proofed.

Hot tip

If you buy a PCI-Express device, make sure it supports the latest version of the interface – currently version 3.0.

Hot tip

There is also a version of the SATA interface designed specifically for external hard drives. This is known as eSATA and it provides data transfer speeds similar to the SATA interface.

...cont'd

Don't forget

Provided a high level of performance is not required, motherboards offering integrated sound and video systems are a good way for the upgrader to cut costs.

Hot tip

Bluetooth is a technology that allows short-range wireless communication between suitably equipped devices. These can be mice, keyboards, printers, scanners, etc. Currently, it is rare to see a Bluetooth equipped PC. However, with the present trend towards wireless devices, its popularity is expected to grow.

Integrated Hardware

Traditionally, built-in hardware has been restricted mainly to sound and video systems, neither of which offered much in the way of quality and features. For example, early integrated video did not have 3D capability, which is essential for the playing of 3D games, and the sound systems could only handle the two nasty little speakers that manufacturers, typically, supplied.

Today, the situation is much different. The sound systems now supplied with motherboards can support multiple-speaker setups, and the video systems have full 3D capabilities. For most users, these systems are more than adequate.

Quite apart from sound and video, motherboards offer a range of integrated hardware such as Ethernet and wireless network adaptors, and firewalls.

The advantages these offer to the upgrader are:

● Reduced cost – for example, buying a motherboard with an integrated video system will cost less than buying a motherboard and a separate video card

● Increased expansion options – if some of your hardware is built-in to the motherboard, you will have spare expansion sockets that would be otherwise occupied. These can be used for other devices

Technology

Whatever the reason for replacing a motherboard, the act of doing so presents an ideal opportunity to also embrace more recent PC technologies. For example:

● CPU technology, such as multi-core processors

● System interfaces, such as SATA, PCI-Express, USB 3 and Bluetooth

● DDR3 memory

● Dual- and triple-channel memory configurations

Modern motherboards (high-end models, in particular) also provide a range of useful features. We'll take a look at some of these on the next page.

Motherboard Features

Multi-Channel Memory

Traditionally, motherboards have provided just one memory channel, which usually results in the system's memory having insufficient bandwidth to keep pace with the CPU, thus creating a data bottleneck.

Dual- and triple-channel motherboards provide extra channels, which effectively double or treble the bandwidth available to the memory. With two or three channels working simultaneously, the bottleneck can be reduced considerably. Rather than wait for memory technology to improve, multi-channel architecture takes the existing technology and enhances the way it is utilized.

Dual-Video Card Setups

For the ultimate in graphics performance, the two main graphics card manufacturers, AMD/ATI and Nvidia, both provide a dual-video card setup. Nvidia's is called SLI (Scalable Link Interface) and AMD/ATI's is known as CrossFire. These employ matched pairs of video cards that operate in tandem to produce vastly improved 3D graphics performance. Their main use, not surprisingly, is PC gaming. The frame rate in games can be doubled, while the games can be run at higher, more detailed resolutions without loss of performance.

These setups require a motherboard equipped with two video card sockets.

The BIOS

While all motherboards provide a BIOS chip, some of them provide many more features than others. These can include:

- A RAID setup utility with which to configure two or more hard drives for performance gains or data protection

- A quick boot utility that speeds up the PC's boot up time

- An over-clocking utility, which enables users to get more performance from their CPU and memory

- A backup utility that creates an image of the system, which can be used to restore the system to exactly how it was in the event of a major failure

Replacing a Motherboard

The motherboard is the large circuit board screwed to the right-hand panel of the system case. Before it can be replaced with a new model, you will have to remove it. Do this as follows:

- Disconnect all the cables connected to it. These will be the motherboard and CPU power supplies from the PSU, the drive (hard drive, DVD drive, floppy drive) interface cables, and the front panel port cables

- Remove all expansion boards such as video cards, etc

- Undo the six screws that secure the motherboard and remove it from the case

- Remove the input/output shield

- In many cases, the power supply unit (PSU) will also have to be removed as it will block access to the board

With the old board out of the way, fit the new one as described below:

Don't forget

Remember to replace the input/output shield. This stops objects being poked through, which may damage the motherboard, or kiddies fingers, which may damage the kiddie.

Fit the new input/output shield. This clips into place from the inside

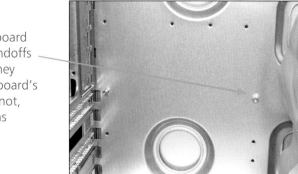

Hold the new board against the standoffs to make sure they align with the board's screw holes. If not, relocate them as necessary

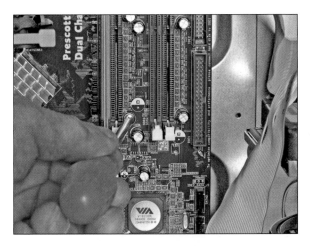

Secure the board with the supplied screws

Connect the board's power supplies from the PSU, and the drive interface cables

Connect the cables for the case switches, speaker, and front panel LEDs

Configuring the BIOS

When the system is back in one piece, certain configuration settings in the BIOS may need to be changed. These are done via the BIOS setup program, which is accessed by pressing a key as the PC boots (the key will be specified at the bottom of the first boot screen), as shown below:

Hot tip

The key required to enter the BIOS setup program will be specified on the boot screen. It should also be specified in the documentation.

```
Phoenix - AwardBIOS v6.00PC, An Energy Star Ally
Copyright © 1984-2003, Phoenix Technologies, Ltd

KM266M.B12 For KM266-MNB

Main Processor : AMD Athlon 1200Mhz
Memory Testing : 262144K OK

     Primary Master : ST340014A 3.54
      Primary Slave : None
   Secondary Master : LITE-ON LTR-52327S QSOB
    Secondary Slave : None




Press Del to enter SETUP
10/09/2003-KM266-8235-6A6LVP8CC-00
```

BIOS setup program entry key (DEL)

Navigating the BIOS is done using the following keys:

Don't forget

To move around in the BIOS, use the Esc and arrow keys. Settings are changed with the Page Up and Page Down keys. The Enter key confirms the change.

- Up arrow key – moves the cursor up

- Down arrow key – moves the cursor down

- Left arrow key – moves the cursor left

- Right arrow key – moves the cursor right

- Page Up key – selects a higher value

- Page Down key – selects a lower value

- Enter key – make a selection

- Escape key – return to the previous menu

Enabling USB

In most BIOSs, USB is disabled by default. Enable it as follows:

1 On the main BIOS page, select Integrated Peripherals and press Enter

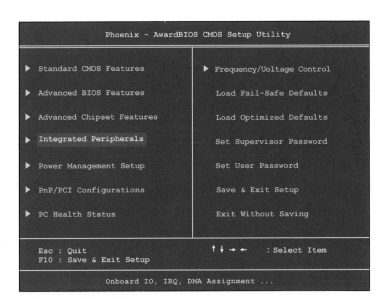

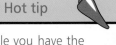
While you have the Integrated Peripherals screen open, scroll down and check to see if your board provides USB 3. If it does, you will see an Onboard USB 3.0 Controller option. Make sure this is enabled as well.

2 Scroll to USB Controllers and press Enter to open the Options screen. Select Enabled and then press Enter to confirm the selection and return to the main screen

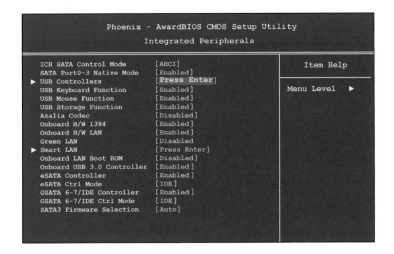

...cont'd

Setting Up a Video Card

If you have a video card in your system, this needs to be set up in the BIOS by specifying what interface it uses.

If you are using a video system integrated in the motherboard, you can skip this step.

1   Enter the BIOS program and on the main BIOS page, select Advanced BIOS Features

2   Scroll to "Init Display First" and press Enter. A new menu will open from which you can select the relevant option (AGP, PCI, PCIE x16, etc). Press Enter again to confirm the selection and return to the previous screen

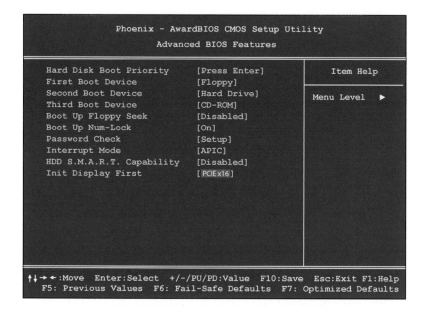

Note that motherboards usually denote the PCI-Express x16 option as PCIE x16. In some boards it may be denoted as PEG.

Also, if your motherboard has two or more PCI-Express x16 slots, you will have options for PCIE x16-1, PCIE x16-2, PCIE x16-3, etc. The figure at the end identifies the slot and the 1 socket will be the topmost on the board, the 2 slot the next one down, and so on. Make sure you select the socket the card is installed in.

Disabling Integrated Sound

All motherboards come with the integrated sound system enabled by default in the BIOS. If you intend to use a sound card, you must disable it, otherwise the card will not work.

1. Open the Integrated Peripherals page and locate the entry that relates to the motherboard's integrated sound. In the screenshot below, it is the Azalia codec but this will probably be different in your board. If in doubt, the motherboard's manual will specify what to look for

2. Scroll to the appropriate setting, which will currently be Enabled, and press Enter to open the Options screen. Select Disabled and press Enter again.

Don't forget

If you are planning to use a sound card in your computer, it will be necessary to disable the motherboard's integrated sound system.

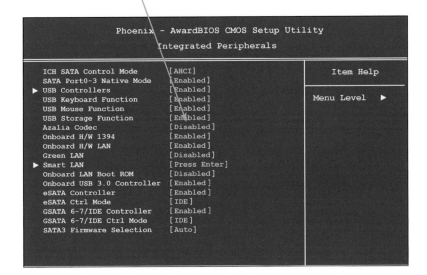

```
              Phoenix - AwardBIOS CMOS Setup Utility
                      Integrated Peripherals

   ICH SATA Control Mode      [AHCI]              Item Help
   SATA Port0-3 Native Mode   [Enabled]
 ▶ USB Controllers            [Enabled]
   USB Keyboard Function      [Enabled]        Menu Level    ▶
   USB Mouse Function         [Enabled]
   USB Storage Function       [Enabled]
   Azalia Codec               [Disabled]
   Onboard H/W 1394           [Enabled]
   Onboard H/W LAN            [Enabled]
   Green LAN                  [Disabled]
 ▶ Smart LAN                  [Press Enter]
   Onboard LAN Boot ROM       [Disabled]
   Onboard USB 3.0 Controller [Enabled]
   eSATA Controller           [Enabled]
   eSATA Ctrl Mode            [IDE]
   GSATA 6-7/IDE Controller   [Enabled]
   GSATA 6-7/IDE Ctrl Mode    [IDE]
   SATA3 Firmware Selection   [Auto]
```

Please note that when you make changes to settings in the BIOS the changes need to be saved. You will find the option for this on the main page (alternatively, press the F10 key). If you don't save them, the settings will revert to the original ones when you exit the BIOS.

Upgrading the BIOS

The BIOS is responsible for initializing the PC's bootup procedure, and recognizing and configuring the system's hardware prior to the loading of the operating system.

Like every other part of the computer, the development of new technology renders the BIOS program out-of-date. Fortunately, modern BIOSs can be upgraded by means of a flash utility (see margin note).

But how do you know when your BIOS needs upgrading? The answer is when you need to run software or a hardware device that uses technology not supported by the BIOS. A good example of this is when one of the new solid state drives is installed. These devices require an up-to-date BIOS in order to perform at their best. The following are some more examples:

● CPU support – the BIOS enables the motherboard to accept CPUs up to a certain speed, or of a certain type. In many cases, older motherboards can be made compatible with more recent CPUs by a BIOS upgrade

● Large hard drive support – due to inherent limitations, older BIOSs may recognize only part of a hard drive's total capacity. For example, many older BIOSs cannot recognize more than 137.4 GB. So a user buying a 200 GB drive may have the frustration of being unable to use a third of it. One solution to this problem is to upgrade the BIOS

● Bug fixes – all software contains errors; BIOS programs are no different. By making upgrades available, manufacturers are able to offer fixes

Performing a BIOS Upgrade

Having decided that there is a need to upgrade the BIOS, proceed as follows:

1) The first step is to correctly identify the model number of both the motherboard and the BIOS chip

Hot tip

Modern BIOSs are flash upgradable, which means that the instructions they contain can be overwritten with updated versions. To do it, you need the update file, which is available from the motherboard's manufacturer, and a flash utility.
   Note that many older BIOSs are not upgradable.

Beware

The most critical part of BIOS upgrading is getting the correct update file. To this end, you must be able to correctly identify the manufacturer and model number of both the BIOS and the motherboard.

2) Locate and obtain the BIOS update file. This will be available at the motherboard manufacturer's website. You will also need an upgrading utility. These are known as "flash" utilities and will also be available from the motherboard manufacturer

3) Double-click the downloaded BIOS file (this is usually in a zipped format) and extract the contents to a blank CD or DVD. If a flash utility isn't included, you'll have to copy one to the disk as well

4) Now make the disk bootable. Most disk burning utilities, such as Nero and Roxio Creator, provide an option for doing this

5) Place the boot disk in the CD/DVD drive and restart the PC. When the PC has booted up, the flash utility should open automatically. From this point on, you will have to follow the instructions included with the utility as the procedure varies according to the utility used. Typically though, it involves little more than simply typing in the name of the update file and its location, and then pressing Enter

Hot tip

Some motherboard manufacturers provide a BIOS upgrade utility built-in to the BIOS. Details will be in the computer documentation.

Others provide a Windows based utility, which can be downloaded from their website or may be on the motherboard installation disc. Download it to your PC, click a button, and the upgrade will be downloaded and installed with no further input from the user. This is the easiest and safest way to do the job.

A typical BIOS flash utility

Hot tip

Most upgrade utilities allow the user to make a backup of the existing BIOS instructions. In the event of problems, this can be used to restore the original BIOS settings.

Upgrading System Interfaces

A PC's interface (also known as a BUS) is a communication channel that passes data to and from its components. Think of it as a road system with the individual components all having their own address on the road and you'll get the picture.

Different parts of the system use different types of interface, e.g. the front side bus for data transfer between the motherboard, the CPU and memory, the SATA interface for the system's drives, the PCI-Express x16 interface for video, etc.

As computer technology advances, interfaces (and hence the devices that use them) become obsolete and are replaced with new ones. Thus, upgraders may find that their system is not compatible with the interface used by modern devices. Some, such as the motherboard's FSB, cannot be upgraded without replacing the motherboard.

However, there are others that can. These are the ones that are used to connect external devices, such as printers, scanners, etc. Internal hard drive interfaces can be upgraded as well.

All that's necessary is to buy an expansion card that provides the appropriate interface technology and ports, and install it in an expansion socket on the motherboard.

Here we have a card that provides two USB 3 ports, and also two FireWire ports

This card adds the SATA 3 drive interface to the system

5 Store More On Your PC

In this chapter, we look at the PC's main data storage device – the hard drive. You'll learn about the various interfaces used by these devices and important specifications – factors that need to be considered when buying a drive.

Hard Drives

Hard drives are one of the components most likely to fail in a computer system. This is because they are mechanical devices that use motors, bearings and other moving parts. Inevitably, these parts are subject to wear and tear and will eventually fail. When a hard drive does fail, it is almost always terminal – these devices cannot usually be repaired. Any data that was on the drive will be lost.

70

Unfortunately, they also happen to be one of the more difficult components to upgrade. The physical installation is easy enough (just four screws and two cables – interface and power). What's not quite so straightforward is preparing them for use by partitioning and formatting.

Furthermore, if the drive being replaced is the main system drive on which is loaded the operating system, then this will have to be re-installed, as will any programs installed on it.

Yet another complication is choosing the best type of drive for your purposes, e.g. SCSI, SATA, etc.

The following pages explain everything you need to know to carry out a hard drive upgrade successfully.

Does it Need Upgrading?

There are three reasons to upgrade a hard drive:

1) The existing drive has failed, or is beginning to fail
2) To take advantage of more recent drive technology
3) More storage capacity is needed

In the first two instances, there is nothing to think about – the drive has to be replaced. In the latter case, however, an upgrade may not be necessary.

If you've been using your drive for some time and have now run out of space, it could be time to simply have a clear-out and get rid of redundant data. The quickest and easiest way to do this is as follows:

1 Go to Start, All Programs, Accessories, System Tools, and Disk Cleanup

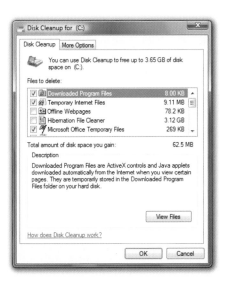

2 Select the drive to be cleaned up. After a few moments, you will be presented with a list of files that can be safely deleted. Make your selection by checking the appropriate boxes and click OK

Clicking the More Options tab gives you three more options:

1) The removal of Windows components that are not used
2) The removal of third-party programs that are not used
3) The deletion of System Restore files (see margin note)

Work through these and delete as much stuff as you can. This should free up enough hard drive space to cover most purposes, particularly if you had a lot of System Restore files.

Beware

The following are all signs of a hard drive that's on the way out, and need to be acted upon if you don't want to lose all your data:

• Unusual levels of mechanical noise

• The PC locks-up frequently

• File system errors (indicated by Chkdsk)

• Spurious loss of data

Hot tip

Those of you running versions of Windows from Me onwards have a utility known as System Restore. This is used to restore the system to a previous state in the event of problems, and it works by taking a snapshot of the system at periodic intervals and saving it as a file. These files can be huge, and a number of them can occupy several gigabytes of hard drive space.

Hard Drive Interfaces

Having made the decision to upgrade your hard drive, your next decision is what type of drive to go for.

A hard drive interface is the technology used to connect the drive to the system. There are several drive interfaces, all of which offer different data transfer rates and features. Some are designed for internal drives and some for external drives.

Note that hard drives are classified according to the interface they are designed to use, e.g. a drive that uses the SATA interface is known as a SATA drive.

The issue of data transfer rates can be very confusing for the uninitiated as they are commonly quoted in two different metrics. For example, a FireWire drive is quoted at 800 Mbps, and a SATA drive is quoted at 300 MBps. Which is the faster?

Most people will think it's the FireWire drive and they will be wrong because Mbps is an abbreviation for Megabits per second, while MBps is an abbreviation for Megabytes per second. 800 Mbps equates to 100 MBps, so in the example above the SATA drive is three times as fast as the FireWire drive.

In this chapter, we'll be using Megabytes per second (MBps) as this is the metric used by Windows operating systems and so will be the one most familiar to users.

Serial ATA (SATA)

SATA is a development of the PATA (Parallel Advanced Technology Attachment) interface and has now superseded it to become the mainstream internal hard drive interface. Virtually all drives fitted in consumer PCs use this interface.

There are several versions of SATA: The original, SATA 150, has a data transfer rate of 150 MBps, the second, SATA 300, transfers data at 300 MBps, and the third, SATA 600, has a transfer rate of 600 MBps.

Of the three, SATA 300 is currently the de facto version. SATA 600 will eventually take over but at the moment offers a level of performance that very few users need. Also, SATA 600 compatible motherboards are relatively scarce, plus they are more expensive.

Hot tip

Note that the figures quoted in data transfer rate specifications are theoretical maximums that can only be achieved under ideal operating conditions. In practice, this is almost never achieved and actual transfer rates are considerably less.

External SATA (eSATA)

The eSATA interface is basically an extension of SATA and is used to connect external hard drives. Prior to its introduction,

external drives used either FireWire or USB 2, both of which have considerably slower data transfer rates than the SATA 300 interface. eSATA, which operates at the same speed as SATA 300, enables external drives to run at the same speed as an internal SATA hard drive.

Universal Serial Bus (USB)

USB is a system interface that is similar in concept to FireWire. It enables up to 127 devices to run simultaneously on a computer and has many of the features offered by FireWire, such as hot-swapping, plug-and-play and power provision.

USB currently comes in two versions – USB 2, which has a data transfer speed of 57 MBps, and the much faster USB 3, which has a transfer rate of 572 MBps.

Of the two, USB 2 is currently the mainstream standard and will be found on all motherboards built from 2004 onwards. Virtually all the USB devices in current use are designed to use this version.

TM & © 2008 USB-IF. All rights reserved.

The recent introduction of USB 3, which is not only ten times as fast as USB 2 but also offers many other technological advances, has probably sounded the death knell for FireWire and eSATA. Not only is it much faster, it does everything FireWire and eSATA do, and more. As a result, new motherboards may soon be offering USB 3 only, as by doing so the manufacturers will be able to cut their costs.

With regard to hard drives, USB is only used by external models.

Hot tip

USB 2 is sometimes referred to as Highspeed USB, and USB 3 is sometimes referred to as Superspeed USB.

73

Hot tip

USB 3 is some ten times faster than USB 2. So if you decide on a USB hard drive, get one that supports USB 3. Your system probably won't be able to make use of the extra speed but it's pointless buying into yesterday's technology.

...cont'd

FireWire

FireWire (also known as IEEE 1394 and iLink), is a system interface that comes in two versions: FireWire 400, with a data transfer rate of 50 MBps, and FireWire 800, with a transfer rate of 100 MBps.

As with USB and eSATA, this interface is used to connect external devices and, for a considerable period, its characteristics made it the best available interface for this purpose. It was commonly used on video equipment such as camcorders, and external hard drives.

However, with the advent of USB 2, its popularity has waned somewhat. While current external drives still offer it, usually with USB 2 as well, modern video equipment has switched over to USB 2 and HDMI.

Small Computer System Interface (SCSI)

As with USB and FireWire, SCSI is a system interface that is not limited just to disk drives – it can also be used for printers, scanners, etc.

SCSI has been around for a long time now, which is a testament to its capabilities. It is a very fast interface having a maximum data transfer rate of 320 MBps, and is extremely reliable. Also, devices in a SCSI setup can carry out actions without having to involve the main system processor. This reduces system overhead, increases efficiency and results in lower power usage.

These factors, plus others, make it ideally suited for running large numbers of hard drives in corporate and server environments.

Serial Attached SCSI (SAS)

SAS is basically a much improved version of SCSI and offers a data transfer rate of 600 MBps. With this interface, every drive in the system has a dedicated channel, unlike SCSI where all the drives have to share one channel.

SAS interface cables are also narrower than SCSI cables, which makes them easier to route and also improves airflow in the system case.

As with SCSI, the advantages provided by SAS are particularly relevant in business environments.

Don't forget

The SCSI and SAS interfaces are not supported by mainstream motherboards, which means an adapter has to be installed.

Types of Hard Drive

As with interfaces, there are various types of hard drive. Most of them are named after the interface they use, hence we have SATA, eSATA, SCSI, SAS, USB and FireWire drives.

While the above are all mechanical devices and use the same basic electro-magnetic technology, they each have strengths that make them suitable for specific applications and weaknesses that render them less suitable for others.

A recent development in hard drive technology is Solid State Drives (SSDs). These devices have no moving parts, are compact and rugged, and offer blindingly fast performance.

We'll start with hard drives designed for internal use.

SATA Drives
Internal SATA drives are currently the hard drive of choice for the vast majority of PC owners. While they are not the best type of drive, they offer the most practical storage solution in terms of performance versus cost.

Low-end to mid-range SATA drives use the SATA 300 interface, which provides a very healthy maximum data transfer rate of 300 MBps. Models in this class, typically, have a rotational or spindle speed of 7200 rpm, a buffer size of 8-32 MB, and a seek time of around 8.5 seconds.

In terms of reliability, these drives have a typical rating of 50,000 Stop/Start Cycles, and an MTBF (Mean Time Between Failures) rating of around 1,000,000 hours.

At the high-end of the SATA market, drives use the SATA 600 interface (600 MBps data transfer rate), have a rotational speed of 10,000 rpm, a buffer size of 32-64 MB, and a seek time of 3.5 seconds. The reliability specs are 600,000 Start/Stop cycles and a MTBF of 1,500,000.

SATA hard drives are currently available in capacities of up to 3 TB (3000 GB).

SCSI Drives
SCSI drives have long been the hard drive favored for applications that demand the highest levels of performance and reliability.

Hot tip

If you are not looking for anything out of the ordinary with respect to your hard drive, a SATA 300 model is the obvious choice. It will provide good performance at a sensible price.

This is due to the fact that these drives have an extremely high build quality while at the same time being capable of fast data transfer rates (320 MBps) due to use of the SCSI interface.

SCSI drives have a rotational speed of 15,000 rpm, a buffer size of 16 MB, and a seek time of 3.5 seconds. Reliability figures are 600,000 Start/Stop cycles and a MTBF of 1,500,000.

The drawbacks of SCSI drives are that storage capacity is limited to around 300 GB, and that the high spindle speed makes them considerably more noisy in operation than SATA drives. Also, mainstream motherboards do not provide the SCSI interface, which means that if a user wants to use one of these drives, an SCSI adapter card will have to be installed. This further increases the cost of an already expensive setup.

SAS Drives

SAS drives are essentially the same as SCSI models but the use of the SAS interface enables them to offer improved performance.

Rotational speed, buffer size, seek time, and reliability specifications are much the same as with SCSI drives. However, the SAS interface enables a maximum data transfer rate of up to 600 MBps.

While these drives are also noisy due to the high spindle speeds, and expensive; they do offer much higher storage capacities than SCSI drives of up to 1 TB. As with SCSI drives, a SAS adapter card will have to be installed as mainstream motherboards do not provide the SAS interface.

SSD Drives

Solid state drives are the latest thing to hit the hard drive market. These devices use solid state memory to store data and thus contain no moving parts which, quite apart from anything else, makes them extremely reliable.

The key components of an SSD are the memory chips (non-volatile flash memory), and a processor that acts as a controller. Incorporated into the controller is the interface that connects the drive to the PC, and this is usually SATA 300. SSDs that use the SATA 600 interface are just beginning to hit the market at the time of writing. A few use PCI-Express x4.

SSDs offer many advantages over traditional mechanical drives. For example:

- SSDs start instantaneously; HDDs take several seconds

- SSD access time is about 0.1 ms; HDD access time ranges from 3.5 to 10 ms

- SSD read performance is consistent, whereas with HDDs it varies according to the level of drive fragmentation

- SSDs are completely silent in operation as they have no moving parts

- No moving parts makes SSDs almost 100 per cent reliable All HDDs are prone to mechanical and heat issues

- SSDs are much smaller and lighter than HDDs

- SSDs require much less power than HDDs

However, there are issues with these devices: One is their cost – an SSD costs about $2.00 per GB while a mechanical hard drive costs about ten cents per GB – 20 times as expensive.

Another is that low-end models have a write speed (typically, 50 MBps) that is no better than that of a mechanical hard drive. While their read speed can be as high as 350 MBps, they don't move data any faster than an ordinary HDD. This limitation does not apply to the high-end models though, which have write speeds similar to their read speeds.

SSDs also require a bit more attention during the installation procedure than mechanical drives do. Furthermore, changes need to be made to the operating system's default settings in order to get, and maintain, the best performance from them. We look at this on pages 91-92.

Beware

Another drawback of SSDs is that their performance degrades over time. To combat this, a technology known as TRIM is used and, currently, only the very latest operating systems support it.

...cont'd

H-HHD Drives

A hybrid hard drive is basically a SATA mechanical drive, which also incorporates a cache (typically 3 or 4 GB in size) of the same type of flash memory used in SSDs.

In operation, frequently used data is stored in the flash memory and because the seek time of flash memory is so fast, when the data is accessed again, the drive's response is almost as fast as that of an SSD.

In operation these drives approach the speed of an SSD while, at the same time, providing much greater, and much cheaper, storage capacity. In terms of overall performance, a modern hybrid drive slots in between high-end 10,000 rpm SATA drives and solid-state drives.

Needless to say, there are drawbacks. A hybrid drive spins-up and spins-down more often than a normal hard drive, which results in greater mechanical wear and tear, and hence a shorter working life. This can also increase noise levels.

It should also be noted that hybrid drives are designed for use with laptops and, accordingly, have the 2.5 inch form factor. However, they can be used in a Desktop PC with a suitable mounting bracket.

External Hard Drives

Hard drives designed to be used externally come in two types – Desktop with a 3.5 inch form factor, and Portable with a 2.5 inch form factor. Both types use the same SATA technology found in mainstream SATA internal drives.

The only differences are that external models are supplied in a protective case or enclosure, and that some need a separate power supply.

As regards interfaces, most of them use both USB 2 (recent models USB 3), and FireWire 800, while others use eSATA.

Currently, the highest capacity for a single drive is 3 TB. However, for those who need even more storage than this, external drive enclosures are available with two, or more, 3 TB drives configured in a RAID 0 setup for increased performance.

Hot tip

External hard drives come pre-partitioned and formatted. Simply plug them in and they're ready to go.

Hot tip

External drives are available in "tough case" models that are built to withstand being dropped and otherwise physically abused.

Buying a Hard Drive

By now you should have a good idea of what to look for when buying a drive for your new system. If you're still unsure, however, the following may help:

Of all the components in a computer system, the one that most needs to be of high quality is the hard drive because this is where all a user's data is kept. While even low-end drives provide a performance level that is more than adequate for most users, their build quality, and hence reliability, are not acceptable when mission-critical data needs to be stored. In this type of environment, the choice has to be an SCSI or SAS drive. This will be expensive though as both of these drives require an adapter card to be fitted, and these can be as expensive as the drive itself.

The intended use of the PC also has a big bearing on the choice of hard drive. Applications such as gaming, video, CAD, etc, all require a highly specified PC. Putting a low-end drive into such a system will effectively drag all the high quality components down to its level. To get the best out of these types of application, a SATA 600 drive with a spindle speed of 10,000 rpm, or an SSD will be necessary. For more general, less demanding use, a SATA 300 drive will be fine.

Don't get too bogged down with hard drive specifications. These can be misleading (sometimes deliberately so) and in many cases lead buyers into assumptions that are incorrect. Be aware that the drive manufacturers use specification sheets as marketing tools, and the figures they quote are invariably taken under ideal operating conditions that can never be achieved in practice.

Many users have steered clear of external hard drives in the past as they have traditionally been much slower than internal models. This is no longer the case however, as drives using the eSATA and USB 3 interfaces are every bit as fast. While you will need an internal drive for the operating system and your applications, an external drive as well is ideal for extra storage, and more importantly, as an independent backup medium.

If performance and/or reliability are important but you can't afford a high-end SAS/SCSI drive, consider buying two standard SATA 300 drives and setting them up in a RAID 0 (performance) or RAID 1 (reliability) configuration. See pages 82-83 for more on this subject.

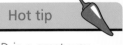

Hot tip

RAID is a great way of configuring a combination of hard drives to gain specific benefits. Depending on the RAID configuration chosen, these can be performance, reliability, or both.

Installing a Hard Drive

As the vast majority of upgraders will buy a SATA drive, this is what we'll use here to demonstrate the installation procedure.

At the front of the case, you'll see the drive cages. The wider cage at the top is for your CD/DVD drive; the narrower cage below is where the hard drive goes.

In low-end cases, the drive will probably have to be secured by four screws. Better cases usually provide a tool-free method of securing the drive. Whichever, having done so, connect it to the system as shown below:

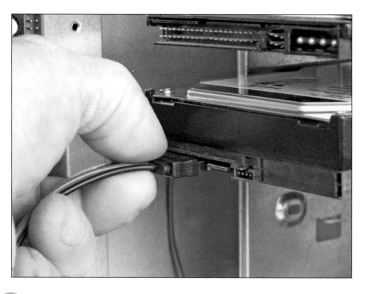

1 Take a SATA power connector from the Power Supply Unit and connect it to the drive's power socket. This is situated at the rear-left of the drive

If your Power Supply Unit does not provide SATA power connectors (likely if you are using an older model), you can buy adapters that convert the Molex power connector found in older PSUs to SATA. An example is shown below:

SATA connector  Molex connector

2 Connect one end of the interface cable to the socket at the right of the power supply socket

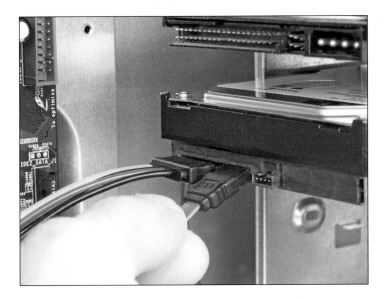

Hot tip

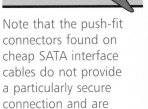

Note that the push-fit connectors found on cheap SATA interface cables do not provide a particularly secure connection and are easily dislodged. Our recommendation is to pay a bit more for cables that have a locking clip.

3 Connect the other end to a SATA socket on the motherboard

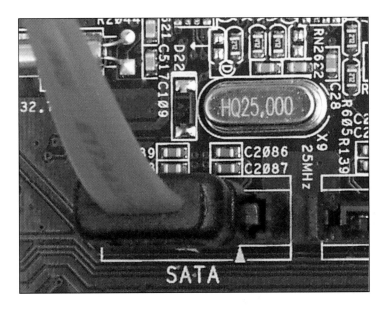

Hot tip

The motherboard will provide several SATA sockets. These will be labeled SATA 1, SATA 2, etc. You can install as many drives as there are sockets.

RAID Configurations

RAID is a way of configuring a combination of hard drives to gain specific benefits, and it requires at least two drives. For the budget conscious upgrader, it is a great way to turn two (or more) drives of average quality into one high-performance drive or, alternatively, into a drive offering a high level of data protection.

Of the various RAID configurations, the ones described below may be of interest in a home-PC environment.

RAID 0

This requires a minimum of two drives, (preferably identical) and works by splitting (known as striping) the data equally between them. The result is much improved data transfer speeds (up to 50 per cent) as each drive handles part of a file simultaneously.

RAID 1

This also requires a minimum of two drives. In this configuration, all data saved is duplicated (known as mirroring) on each drive. The purpose is data protection – if one drive fails, the data is recoverable from the other/s.

RAID 0/1

This is a combination of RAID 0 and RAID 1 and requires a minimum of four drives. Half the drives are used to stripe the data, and the other half to mirror it. Thus, it provides fast data transfer, together with data protection.

RAID 5

This requires a minimum of three drives. Data is striped across all the drives but an error checking bit (known as the parity bit) is also stored. Should any one drive fail, the RAID controller will calculate the missing data (using the parity bit) and keep the system running until the faulty drive can be replaced.

To implement RAID, you need a RAID controller, which sets up and maintains the configuration. This will be provided by the motherboard in the form of a software integrated controller.

Alternatively, you can install a hardware based RAID controller card (shown left) if you want a higher quality RAID setup. The software based controllers provided by motherboards are perfectly adequate for home PC use, however. The next page shows how it's done.

Hot tip

Note that with RAID 0, the capacity of the setup will be the sum of the drives, e.g. two 320 GB drives will be seen by Windows as a single drive with a capacity of 640 GB.

With RAID 1, the capacity of one of the drives is lost so using the example above, Windows will see one drive with a capacity of 320 GB.

The method of creating a RAID array depends on your hardware. High-end motherboards usually provide a Windows RAID utility that allows the user to install the operating system on a single drive and then create and modify the RAID array from Windows.

Most motherboards however, do not provide this facility in which case it has to be done in the BIOS. The instructions for how to access the BIOS RAID utility will be in the motherboard manual. When you open the utility, you will see something similar to the screenshot below:

Beware

Software RAID controllers as provided by motherboards are not as reliable as hardware RAID controller cards. They also offer lower performance levels.

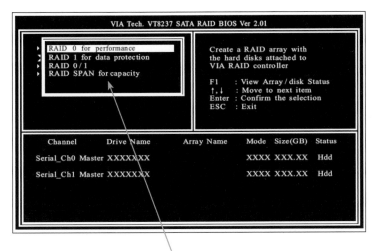

Typically, you will be given four options: RAID 0, RAID 1, RAID 0/1 and RAID Span. Make your choice and press Enter.

To make the task easier, most BIOS RAID setup utilities offer an auto-setup option. All you have to do is specify the configuration required which, in the example above, is RAID 0. The utility will then set up the configuration automatically; the process taking only a few seconds. Reboot and you're done.

A two-drive RAID 0 setup provides a huge boost in drive speed, typically, 50 per cent. The downside, of course, is that there is a 50 per cent greater chance of losing your data as a result of drive failure. Also, it is not unknown for software based motherboard RAID controllers to malfunction with the same result. This is why a dedicated hardware RAID controller card, which provides a more reliable setup, should be used when your data is mission-critical.

Hot tip

A two-drive RAID 0 setup should provide a performance increase of around 50 per cent. Adding a third drive should increase it by a further 30 per cent, and a fourth drive by about 20 per cent, and so on.

Beware

The danger of a RAID 0 setup is that you have a much greater chance of losing your data due to hard drive failure.

Partitioning and Formatting

An internal hard drive must be partitioned before it can be used. When the partition has been created, it must then be formatted. The latter process organizes it into logical units known as blocks, sectors and tracks. These are used by the operating system to "remember" where data is stored on the drive.

The procedures vary according to which version of Windows you are using and also on whether the drive is to be used purely for extra storage or is going to be the main system drive, i.e. where Windows is installed.

Partitioning and Formatting a Drive to be Used as Extra Storage

This is the more straightforward of the two scenarios as the procedures can be done within Windows. The following applies to Windows XP, Windows Vista and Windows 7.

Hot tip

Drives can be split into a number of partitions, each of which appear to the operating system as a separate hard drive. Alternatively, one partition equal to the entire capacity of the drive can be created (this is the usual setup).

1 Go to Start, Control Panel, Administrative Tools

2 Click Computer Management and then on the left-hand side, click Disk Management

3 After a few moments, the following window will appear

This shows all the hard drives in the system

4 Right-click the drive to be partitioned (Disk 0 in the screenshot on page 84) and click New Simple Volume (volume is Microsoft parlance for a partition). Windows New Simple Volume Wizard will open. Click Next

5 Click Next in the two dialog boxes that follow

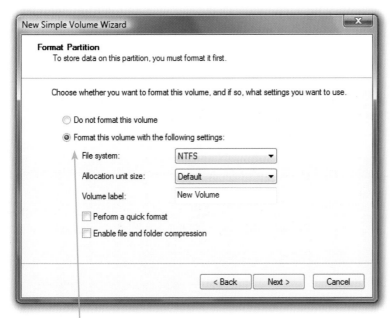

Hot tip

Partitioning is the process of defining specific areas of the hard disk for the operating system to use.
   Formatting prepares a disk to receive data by organizing it into logical units called blocks, sectors and tracks. These enable the drive's read/write heads to accurately position and locate data.

6 Select "Format this volume..." and click Next. Windows will now partition and format the drive. When the procedure is complete, the drive will be available for use

If you now go to My Computer, you will see the drive listed there. If the above procedure is not done the drive won't be recognized by the system and will not show in My Computer.

...cont'd

Partitioning and Formatting a System Drive

By system drive, we mean the drive Windows is installed on. As Windows won't allow you to partition or format the drive it is installed on, the only way to do it is to use the partitioning and formatting tools on the Windows installation disk. Having done so, you will then need to install, or reinstall, Windows.

Before you can do this, the system must be set to boot from the CD/DVD drive. Do this as follows:

1 Restart the PC and enter the BIOS setup program as described previously

2 On the main page, select Advanced BIOS Features and press Enter

Don't forget

To use Windows partitioning and formatting tools, the CD/DVD drive must be set as the first boot device.

```
            Phoenix - AwardBIOS CMOS Setup Utility
                    Advanced BIOS Features

   Virus Warning                [Disabled]         Item Help
   CPU Internal Cache           [Enabled]
   External Cache               [Enabled]       Menu Level    ►
   CPU L2 Cache ECC Checking    [Enabled]
   Quick Power On Self Test     [Enabled]       Select Your Boot
   First Boot Device            [CDROM]         Device Priority.
   Second Boot Device           [HDD-0]
   Third Boot Device            [CDROM]
   Boot Other Device            [Enabled]
   Swap Floppy Drive            [Disabled]
   Boot Up Floppy Seek          [Enabled]
   Bootup NumLock Status        [On]
   Gate A20 Option              [Fast]
   Typematic Rate Setting       [Disabled]
 X Typematic Rate (Chars/Sec)   6
 X Typematic Delay (Msec)       250
   Security Option              [Setup]
   OS Select For Dram > 64MB    [Non-OS2]
   HDD S.M.A.R.T Capability     [Enabled]
```

3 Scroll down to First Boot Device, and using the Page Up/Page Down keys, select CDROM. Save the change and exit the BIOS

Now you can access the drive to partition and format it, and then install Windows. The following procedure does both:

1 Place the Windows installation disk in the CD/DVD drive and then boot the PC

2 When you see a message saying "press any key to boot from CD...", do so

Windows will now load its installation files from the disk. You will then see the following screen:

Hot tip

External hard drives are supplied already partitioned and formatted. Just connect them to the PC and they're ready to go.

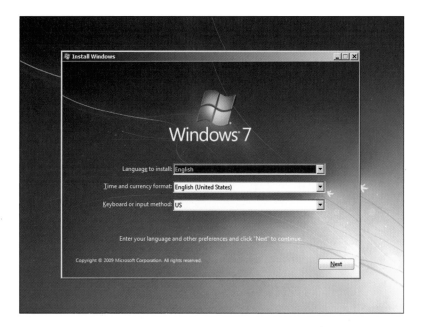

3 Select the required language, and time and currency format, and then click Next. In the screen that opens, click the "Install Now" button.

...cont'd

4 OK the license agreement

5 For the type of installation, select the Custom (advanced) option

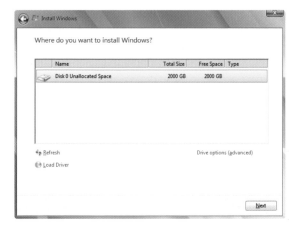

6 In the "Where do you want to install Windows?" screen, you'll see your unformatted and unpartitioned hard drive. Click Drive options (advanced)

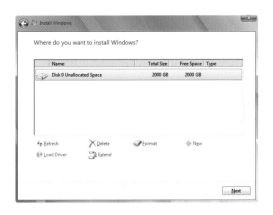

7 Click New

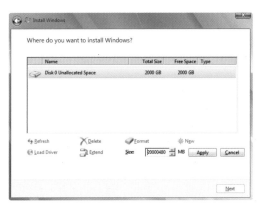

8 Click Apply to create a single partition equal to the size of the drive

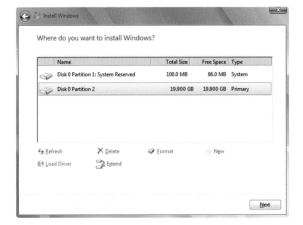

Click Next, and the Windows installation procedure will begin. It should take between 10 and 30 minutes to complete depending on the speed of your PC.

Installing System Drivers

When you run your new installation of Windows for the first time, the first thing to do is complete the installation by installing essential system drivers. The most important of these are the motherboard drivers.

All you have to do is place the motherboard's installation disk in the CD/DVD drive and Windows AutoPlay will automatically open the disk's Setup utility.

Typically, this will give you an easy option, whereby the drivers will be installed along with various other utilities that you may or not want; and an Advanced option, which allows you to choose what is installed.

Hot tip

If in any doubt about what needs to be installed, simply choose the Easy option. While this will install stuff that you probably won't need, it will make sure that what you do need is installed.

To complete the installation of the motherboard's drivers, you will be asked to reboot the PC. When back in Windows, the next step is to install the drivers for any hardware connected to the computer. Typically, these include video cards, sound cards, printers, routers, monitors, mice and keyboards.

Finally, install your programs. While your system is new and performing at its best, we recommend that you benchmark it (see bottom margin note). This will enable you to monitor the system over time, and thus identify any issues that may be causing performance degradation.

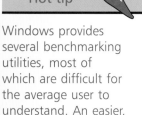

Hot tip

Windows provides several benchmarking utilities, most of which are difficult for the average user to understand. An easier, though less detailed, option is the "Windows Experience Index", which can be accessed by right-clicking Computer in the Start Menu and then clicking Properties. This will show you how Windows rates the main components in your system.

Setting Up an SSD

The characteristics of solid state drives make them particularly suitable for use as a boot drive (the drive Windows is installed on). Using one to provide extra storage space doesn't make any sense as they are so expensive.

Because they work on completely different principles than mechanical hard drives, the installation and, also, maintenance of these devices is somewhat different. If attention is not paid to these factors, the performance of the SSD may be well below what it should be.

Installation

Most current SSDs use the SATA interface and the physical installation is much the same as for a standard SATA hard drive, i.e. they use the same SATA interface cable and power connections. However, as SSDs are considerably smaller than a standard hard drive, they must first be mounted in a bracket so that they can be secured in a 5.25 inch hard drive bay.

Having done this, it is recommended that you then flash upgrade your BIOS to the latest version – see pages 66-67. The reason for doing this is that SSD technology is new and so your existing BIOS may not be able to provide the support that your SSD requires.

The next step is to go into the BIOS and select AHCI mode (IDE is the default mode). Without going into the reasons, SSDs perform much better when operating on AHCI.

see pages 66-67

Don't forget

While you can use an SSD purely for storage, their high price and low storage capacity make them unsuitable for this task. It makes more sense to use them for the boot drive, where their incredible access speeds result in very fast boot times and application launch.

Hot tip

You will find the AHCI setting on the Integrated Peripherals page of the BIOS. If in any doubt, simply change every setting that has an AHCI option to AHCI.

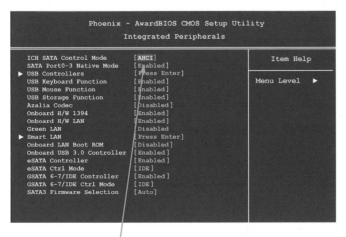

```
          Phoenix - AwardBIOS CMOS Setup Utility
                 Integrated Peripherals

  ICH SATA Control Mode      [AHCI]              Item Help
  SATA Port0-3 Native Mode   [Enabled]
▶ USB Controllers            [Press Enter]
  USB Keyboard Function      [Enabled]         Menu Level  ▶
  USB Mouse Function         [Enabled]
  USB Storage Function       [Enabled]
  Azalia Codec               [Disabled]
  Onboard H/W 1394           [Enabled]
  Onboard H/W LAN            [Enabled]
  Green LAN                  [Disabled]
▶ Smart LAN                  [Press Enter]
  Onboard LAN Boot ROM       [Disabled]
  Onboard USB 3.0 Controller [Enabled]
  eSATA Controller           [Enabled]
  eSATA Ctrl Mode            [IDE]
  GSATA 6-7/IDE Controller   [Enabled]
  GSATA 6-7/IDE Ctrl Mode    [IDE]
  SATA3 Firmware Selection   [Auto]
```

AHCI mode selected

...cont'd

Hot tip

When it is installed on an SSD, the following Windows 7 applications are automatically disabled:

- Defragmentation
- Prefetch
- Superfetch
- Readyboost

Don't forget

If your operating system is not one of the latest, you will probably find that it does not support TRIM. In this case, you will need to get a third-party application to keep your SSD running at peak performance.

With AHCI mode selected, you can now install Windows. Note that Windows 7 is considered the best operating system to use with SSDs as it provides support for the TRIM command and also automatically configures itself to provide the best possible SSD performance.

Maintenance

An issue peculiar to SSDs is that once every memory cell on an SSD has been written to at least once, the performance of the device drops considerably.

To explain this, SSD memory consists of pages. Groups of pages are called blocks. When you delete a file, you are telling the operating system to delete a page on the SSD. However, the page isn't actually deleted – it is merely marked for deletion. This is because data can only be deleted in blocks – single pages can't be deleted.

When the user subsequently saves a file, i.e. requires the space occupied by the "deleted" data, the pages marked for deletion are grouped into a block and the whole block is then wiped clean. Because all this has to happen before the file can be saved, the performance of the SSD is severely undermined.

To overcome this problem, SSDs use what's known as the TRIM command. This is basically an integrated controller that enables the operating system to delete the marked data before the user needs the space, and thus maintains the SSD's performance at a high level.

Because of TRIM, maintenance of SSDs is automatic and requires no input from the user. The only exception to this is when a system is well used, which may result in TRIM struggling to keep up with the constantly changing data on the SSD. To enable it to "keep pace", it is recommended that users let their system idle at the log-on screen for a few hours every week.

Upgraders considering buying an SSD should be aware that only very recent operating systems, such as Windows 7, provide the TRIM command. If an SSD is used with an operating system that doesn't, it will be necessary to acquire a third-party application, such as "wiper.exe" (freely available on the Internet) and run it manually on a frequent basis.

6 Removable Media Options

This chapter looks at various types of drives that provide a more permanent, and thus more reliable, means of data storage than offered by hard drives.

What's Available?

Given the enormous storage capacities offered by today's removable media drives, no self-respecting system can possibly be without one. Their uses are endless – movie and music recording, system backups, data transfer between PCs, etc. The problem is choosing the right type of drive.

Do you settle for a DVD drive or do you splash out for a Blu-ray drive? If you do buy a DVD model, which type do you go for – DVD-ROM, DVD writer or DVD-RAM?

Tape drives, which use cartridges, are ideal for large data backups but do have disadvantages, the main one being the cost of these devices. A more recent, and cheaper, option is a system that uses hard drives as the removable media – these are known as RDX drives.

Then there is the ubiquitous USB flash drive – cheap and cheerful and handy for any number of purposes. Can you tell a good one from a bad one, though?

Your choices are:

- DVD drives
- Blu-ray drives
- RDX drives
- Tape drives
- USB flash drives

We'll start with the most common type of removable media drive – the DVD drive.

Hot tip

Used in conjunction with a suitable backup utility, high-capacity DVDs enable you to make a complete backup of your system.

DVD Drives

DVD (Digital Versatile Disc) drives are very similar in concept to the old and now discontinued CD drives. The basic difference is that DVD drives use a much narrower laser beam for reading and writing, which enables more tracks to be squeezed onto the discs. This vastly increases their storage capacity.

In addition, the composition of a DVD disc allows two layers of data on each side, giving a theoretical maximum of some 17 GB. In practice though, DVD discs currently on sale have a capacity of 4.7 GB, with 8.5 GB (dual-layer) versions also available at a higher price.

Don't forget

DVD discs are available in a dual-layer format, which nearly doubles their storage capacity.

Due to their high storage capacity, DVD discs are used for commercially produced movies, as an entire movie can be stored on one disc. This capacity is also utilized by the PC industry. For example, Microsoft's Encarta Reference Library, which would require five CDs, is available on a single DVD.

The high capacity of DVD discs is handy for PC users as well. Typical applications are system backups and the storage of video, such as TV shows recorded via TV tuner devices.

Another plus for these drives is the fact that they can also read CDs (both software CDs and writable CDs).

DVD drives are available in three versions: read-only (DVD-ROM), writable (DVD-R) and re-writable (DVD-RW).

DVD Formats

The issue of DVD formats also needs to be considered. Currently, there are four of these.

DVD-ROM

Similar to a CD-ROM, discs in this format can only be read – they cannot be written to.

DVD-

This format is supported by Panasonic, Toshiba, Apple, Hitachi, NEC, Pioneer, Samsung and Sharp. It is available in write-once versions (DVD-R) and rewrite versions (DVD-RW).

DVD+

DVD+ is supported by Philips, Sony, Hewlett-Packard, Dell, Ricoh and others. As with DVD-, write-once (DVD+R) and rewrite (DVD+RW) versions are available.

DVD-RAM

A DVD-RAM disc is similar to a hard drive in operation. This format also offers faster data access, and higher levels of reliability than the + and - formats. However, DVD-RAM discs can be read only in a DVD-RAM drive – the format is not generally compatible with DVD+ and DVD- drives.

The table below summarizes the pros and cons of the formats:

Disc	Uses	Pros	Cons
DVD-ROM	Commercial movies, PC games, software	Plays on all drives	Cannot be recorded to
DVD-RAM	Data backup	Offers hard drive like operation, and fast data access. Most reliable format	Poor compatibility. Cannot be played on home DVD players. Discs are expensive
DVD-	Good for video and audio Discs, general data backup and transfer	High level of compatibility with other formats and home DVD players	Lower maximum capacity than DVD+ Discs. Write/read speeds are slower than DVD+
DVD+	Good for mixed data Discs. Can also be used for video and audio Discs	Good level of compatibility with home DVD players	Compatibility with other formats and home DVD players less than DVD-

Hot tip

If your primary purpose for buying a DVD drive is long-term data storage, consider one of the DVD-RAM drives. DVD-RAM discs have the highest life expectancy of all the formats. Furthermore, the drives themselves provide data protection facilities, e.g. the marking of bad sectors. These features make DVD-RAM the most reliable format.

Don't forget

The DVD+ format is more advanced than DVD-. It offers faster write speeds, slightly higher Disc capacity, and built-in data correction. However, the format is generally considered to be less compatible with home and car DVD players.

DVD Drive Specifications

Having decided what type of drive/format you want, the next step is to take a closer look at these devices and see what they actually offer. The following specifications are the ones that should be considered.

Interface

The vast majority of drives currently on the market use the SATA interface. They are also available with USB, FireWire, SCSI, and the old ATA interfaces.

Read/Write Speeds

The speed at which a drive reads and writes is indicated by x ratings in the specifications. Usually, these are marked prominently on the packaging, as shown below.

Hot tip

The interface used by the drive is something that you don't need to worry about unless you are looking to "future-proof" your system. All current interfaces are more than capable of running any of the DVD drives on the market at their full potential.

Better quality DVD drives have a typical read speed of 16x, and a write speed of 24x. With low-end models, the figures are about 12x and 8x respectively

Note that when writing to dual-layer discs, and re-writable discs, write speeds are lower.

DVD drives can also read, and write to, CDs. Typical figures for this type of media are read speeds of 48x and write speeds of 40x.

However, for these figures to have any meaning, you need to know what the x represents. In the case of CDs, it represents 150 KBps. So a CD write speed of 40x means that data is written to the disc at a speed of 6.0 MBps (150 x 40).

In the case of DVDs, the x figure represents 1.32 MBps. So a drive writing a DVD at 22x can write data at a rate of 29 MBps.

With Blu-ray drives, the x represents 6.74 MBps, which means a Blu-ray disc written at 12x will have a write speed of 80 MBps.

...cont'd

Writing Mode

A very important factor in the performance of an optical drive is the maintenance of a constant data transfer rate across the entire disc. To achieve this, manufacturers use one of three methods: Constant Linear Velocity (CLV), Zoned Constant Linear Velocity (ZCLV) and Constant Angular Velocity (CAV).

All you need to know here is that budget and mid-range drives use the CLV or ZCLV method, while top-end models use CAV.

Access Time

This is the time needed to locate a specific item of data on the disc. This metric is measured in milliseconds and you should look for a figure no higher than 160 ms (DVDs) and 140 ms (CDs).

Buffer Size

Optical drives use a buffer to ensure that data flows to the disc smoothly and without interruption during the writing process; this helps to eliminate errors. Typically, drives are supplied with a 2 MB buffer and this is the minimum that you should accept. High-quality drives can have buffers as large as 8 MB.

Recommended Media

The build quality of CDs and DVDs varies widely and some drives have trouble with low-quality discs. To enable users to avoid this potential problem, most manufacturers provide a list of media recommended for use with their drives, as shown below:

Recommended Media		(All DVD-RW and CD-RW media is rewritable up to 1,000 times)
DVD+R	16X	Taiyo Yuden, Verbatim/Mitsubishi
	8X, 4X	Maxell, Ricoh, Taiyo Yuden, Verbatim/Mitsubishi
DVD+RW	4X	Ricoh, Verbatim/Mitsubishi
DVD+R DL	8X, 4X	Verbatim/Mitsubishi
DVD-R	16X, 8X, 4X	Maxell, Taiyo Yuden, TDK, Verbatim/Mitsubishi
DVD-RW	4X, 2X	TDK, Verbatim/Mitsubishi
DVD-R DL	4X	Verbatim/Mitsubishi, Victor
CD-R	48X	Maxell, Taiyo Yuden, TDK
	40X	Ricoh
CD-RW	32X, 24X	Verbatim/Mitsubishi
	10X, 4X	Ricoh, Verbatim/Mitsubishi Chemical

Dual-Layer Discs

A dual-layer disc stores data on both sides, which doubles the maximum storage capacity of a DVD to 8.5 GB. However, these discs can only be written and read by a dual-layer drive. Also, they currently cost more than twice as much as a single-layer DVD, which makes them poor value for money.

Beware

If you are tempted by the high storage capacities offered by dual-layer DVDs, remember that they will be an expensive way of archiving your data.

Blu-ray Drives

Blu-ray drives are most commonly used in consumer electronic devices, such as stand-alone players and games consoles. However, they are also available in the 5.25 inch form factor, which enables them to be internally installed in a computer.

With a wide-screen HD monitor, it is thus possible to watch HD video on the PC. With a capacity of 25 GB, Blu-ray discs are ideal for large-scale backups. So what do you need to look for in a Blu-ray drive designed for PCs?

The first point to make regards the interface these drives use. Currently, they are available in USB, FireWire and SATA versions and, as with hard drives, all of these interfaces are more than capable of handling anything Blu-ray can throw at them. In other words, it doesn't matter which one you go for.

Then there is the issue of price. Drives that can write to a Blu-ray disc are twice as expensive as ones that just read a disc, so if you just want to watch Blu-ray video, buy a read-only model.

With regard to performance, top-end drives have read/write speeds of 10x/12x respectively, while low-end drives can manage only 4x/6x. Access times for top-end drives are around 150 ms, and 250 ms for low-end models.

If you want to use your Blu-ray drive to watch commercial movies on the PC, there are some other requirements apart from the drive itself.

First, the PC must be capable of handling the huge amounts of data that is involved with Blu-ray. This means a dual-core CPU is recommended, with a high-end Pentium or AMD equivalent, being the minimum. With regard to memory, 2 GB is recommended, with 1 GB being the minimum.

A further requirement is that both the video system (be it integrated video or a video card) and the monitor, must be High-Bandwidth Digital Content Protection (HDCP) compliant. If either is not, Blu-ray movies will not play on your PC.

While most recent video cards are HDCP complaint, there are many monitors on the market that are not, so this is an issue that needs to be checked in the specifications.

Hot tip

Blu-ray discs have a current maximum storage capacity of 25 GB. However, future projections are for discs with capacities of up to 200 GB.

Hot tip

With Blu-ray drives, the x represents 6.74 MBps, which means a Blu-ray disc written at 12x will have a write speed of 80 MBps.

Hot tip

High-bandwidth Digital Content Protection (HDCP) is a digital copy protection technology that prevents copying of digital audio and video content.

RDX Drives

Removable Disk Technology (RDX) is a disk-based storage technology that combines the best characteristics of tape drives and hard drives.

An RDX system comprises a docking bay, which can be mounted either externally or internally, and a removable cartridge that is inserted into a slot at the front of the docking bay. The cartridge itself is a standard 2.5 inch (laptop size) SATA 300 hard drive enclosed in a tough shock-resistant casing that is built to withstand physical abuse.

Hot tip

RDX hard drive cartridges are available in capacities of up to 1 TB.

The RDX Quikstor from Tandberg

In operation, when a cartridge is inserted it is immediately detected by the operating system and assigned a drive letter. It can then be used in the same way as any other hard drive.

The advantages of RDX drives include:

Hot tip

When an RDX cartridge is removed from its docking bay, all moving parts within the hard drive are locked in place so no damage can occur during transportation.

- Portability – the cartridge can be quickly removed from the docking bay and slipped into a pocket (a large one)

- Reliability – the cartridge's casing is much tougher than that of an external hard drive or a tape cartridge

- Fast data transfer – as the cartridge is a hard drive, you get the speed and convenience of a hard drive

RDX drives are the ideal solution for those who need to transport large amounts of data easily and securely, and data backups. What really sets them apart from other types of portable drive is the ruggedness of the cartridges and their speed of operation.

Tape Drives

Tape drives are predominantly used in corporate environments and their purpose is to facilitate large-scale system backups. As such, they probably don't have too much relevance to the home PC builder. However, for anyone who may be interested in this type of drive, the following are available:

Digital Audio Tape Drives (DAT)

One of the oldest tape technologies, DAT was originally used for audio recording and uses 4mm tapes (similar in size to the old audio cassettes). These cartridges have a maximum capacity of 80 GB.

The latest version, DAT 320, has a maximum data transfer rate of 24 MBps, which will be seen on top-end models only. Low-end drives can be as slow as 7 MBps.

Digital Linear Tape Drives (DLT)

These devices use both side of the tape which, along with other innovations, vastly increases the amount of data a cartridge can hold (up to 800 GB).

Most DLT drives have a transfer rate of 20 MBps, but top-end models can transfer data at up to 32 MBps.

Linear Tape Open Drives (LTO)

LTO drives are currently the most popular type of tape drive, the reasons for which include: high-capacity cartridges, very fast data transfer rates, and drag & drop capability.

At the low-end, these drives can transfer data at 48 MBps, while at the high-end transfer rates can be as high as 240 MBps. Cartridge capacities range from 400 GB to 1600 GB (1.6 TB).

In general, tape drives are the most expensive type of removable media drive with LTO drives being the most expensive of all. However, once purchased this is mitigated to a certain degree by the relatively low cost of the cartridges. For example, 800 GB cartridges for LTO drives cost in the region of $50.

The big advantage of tape drives is the longevity of the cartridges with most types having a shelf life in the region of 35 years. Also, tape is the most reliable type of storage medium.

USB Flash Drives

A USB flash drive is a device that consists of a circuit board containing a NAND flash memory chip integrated with a USB interface.

These incredibly useful devices have seen off the ubiquitous floppy disk as they are smaller, faster, more robust, use very little power, and have much higher storage capacities.

Beware

Beware of fake USB drives being sold on eBay. Typically, these are the higher capacity models. The give-away is the ridiculously low price being charged. If you see one of these, it's not a bargain, it's a scam.

However, USB flash drives are not all made equal; some are decidedly better than others. While the most obvious difference is their capacity, this is not an indication of quality. To establish the quality of a drive, you need to consider the following factors:

The first is the type of flash memory used – single-level cell (SLC) or multi-level cell (MLC). Without going into the details, SLC is twice as fast as MLC. Furthermore, it lasts ten times as long. However, MLC memory is much cheaper, and so not surprisingly is the type used in most USB flash drives. SLC is only used in top-end drives.

Don't forget

Buyers may also care to look at the software offered with USB flash drives. Useful facilities offered with some are password protection and data encryption.

Unfortunately, the type of memory used is rarely, if ever, mentioned in the specifications. Therefore, buyers need to look at the data transfer rate specification. Low-end models (MLC) have a read speed of about 12 MBps and a write speed of about 5 MBps. High-end drives (SLC) have a read speed of 25 MBps and a write speed of 18 MBps – twice as fast.

Another important consideration with these drives is their build quality. Apart from being slow, cheap models are very flimsy affairs and, while they may work for a while, probably won't last too long. More expensive models on the other hand, are much more rugged in construction, and some of the top-end ones are built to withstand an enormous amount of physical abuse.

Installing an Optical Drive

Below, we see an ATA/IDE DVD drive being installed. The procedure for SATA optical drives is exactly the same as for SATA hard drives – see pages 80-81.

1 Remove the front panel of the system case and then remove the appropriate blanking plate

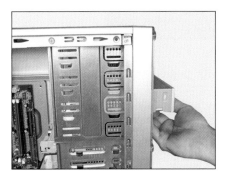

2 Insert the drive from the front (if you try doing it from the back, the PSU may block access) and secure it in place

Hot tip

With modern DVD drives a separate audio cable is not necessary as they use the interface cable to make the connection to the sound system. These drives use a technology called Digital Audio Extraction (DAE).

3 If the drive has an audio cable (see top margin note) to connect it to the sound system, plug one end in the socket at the far left

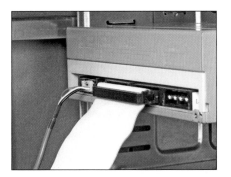

4 Keeping the striped edge to the right, plug the interface cable into the drive

...cont'd

Hot tip

You may need to consult the motherboard or sound card documentation to see where to connect the audio cable.

5 Hook up the power supply

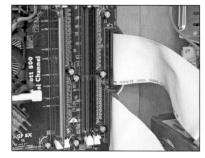 

6 Connect the drive to the ATA socket on the motherboard

7 Connect the audio cable to the sound system

Don't forget

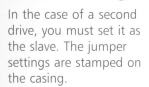

In the case of a second drive, you must set it as the slave. The jumper settings are stamped on the casing.

If you are installing a second ATA/IDE drive, it has to be set as a slave, as shown below. Then as in in step 4 (on the previous page), plug the slave connector into the drive. Otherwise, the procedure is exactly the same.

Then boot the PC and your new drive will now be operational.

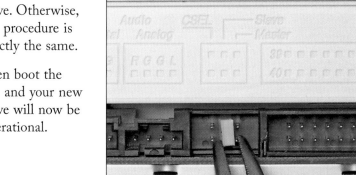

7

See and Hear More With Your PC

In this chapter, we consider the options available to upgraders who want to improve the audio and video capabilities of their PC. In both cases, the upgrader can go for either an integrated solution or a stand-alone device. We look at the pros and cons of both.

Computer Video Systems

Video systems for computers come in two types: integrated video (built-in to the motherboard), and video cards. Both have pros and cons that make them suitable for some purposes and unsuitable for others. It is essential to know what these are in order to get the one most appropriate for your requirements.

Integrated Video Systems

Integrated video is a feature found on the majority of mainstream motherboards (although it is not always used). It is usually incorporated into the chipset and provides a low-cost video option for both users and manufacturers.

Traditionally, however, the quality of video produced by these systems has not been good. On older PCs, it may not even provide 3D, which is essential for many PC games and certain other types of application. However, modern systems do provide a quality of video that is good enough for all but the most demanding applications.

Another problem is the demands made by integrated video on the computer's resources. Video processing needs a powerful processor and a good supply of memory, and integrated video doesn't have either. Thus, the computer's CPU and memory have to be used, with the result that other parts of the system may be short-changed in terms of CPU and memory resources. Overall, system performance is adversely affected.

Reasons to Upgrade

There aren't any. If your PC is no more than four to five years old, your existing integrated system should be capable of handling whatever you throw at it with the possible exception of 3D games, and heavy-duty applications.

Older computers may well benefit. But as the upgrade is going to involve a motherboard replacement, which turns the job into a major upgrade, a much simpler option would be to just add a video card. Even a low-end model that will cost less than a new motherboard will provide you with all the video processing capabilities required.

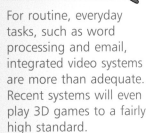

106

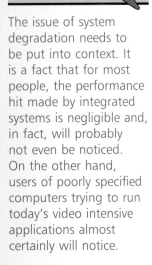

Video Cards

Video cards provide a much higher level of video quality as they are designed specifically for this purpose. To this end they come equipped with their own processor and memory, which means that the system's CPU and memory are free to carry out other unrelated functions. This results in faster overall system performance.

A bonus is the fact that many video cards have integrated functions, which can help to justify the often high cost of these devices. A hardware DVD decoder is a typical example: this will play DVD movies much better than a software decoder.

Bundled software, usually a couple of recent PC games, is often also included in the package.

By providing extra input/output sockets, video cards increase the range of video-related tasks that can be carried out on the PC. Importing video from external devices such as a video recorder is one example of this.

Reasons to Upgrade

There are four reasons to upgrade a video card, or add one:

1) The existing card has failed

2) You start using an application that demands a high level of video-processing

3) To keep abreast of current video technology, such as the PCI-Express interface

4) You need input/output sockets not provided by your existing video system

Beware

The big disadvantage of video cards is the cost. Top-end models that provide the latest technology are almost prohibitive in price. Even mid-range models will make a serious dent in your wallet.

There are also issues regarding the heat these devices produce, the power they use, and the amount of space they occupy.

107

The Video Card Market

When you investigate the video card market, you'll quickly notice that there are a tremendous number of cards on offer, and may wonder how on earth you're going to pick one out.

However, the choice is not nearly as big as it may appear. This is because many of the cards are, to all intents and purposes, identical. The reason for this is that virtually all of them use the same basic architecture – the global processing unit (GPU), otherwise known as the chip.

For example, take the following cards:

- Asus ATI Radeon 5870,
- Sapphire ATI Radeon 5870
- XFX ATI Radeon 5870

Although they are three different cards from three different manufacturers, they are essentially the same because they are all driven, and controlled by, the Radeon 5870 chip. The only differences between them will be in the quality of the manufacturer's control circuitry and the specifications of associated components. For example, the Asus may offer 2 GB of memory, while the Sapphire may have only 1 GB.

The vast majority of the chips used by video card manufacturers are provided by two companies: ATI/AMD (the Radeon) and Nvidia (the GeForce). Note that ATI have recently been taken over by AMD, but many of their products as still advertised as being from ATI.

Both companies offer several versions of each chip they produce – low-end, mid-range and high-end, to cater for different sections of the market. For example, AMD/ATI offers three versions of the Radeon 9800 – the 9800 (low-end), the 9800 PRO (mid-range), and the 9800 XT (high-end).

The differences between the chip versions are determined largely by the following specifications:

- Processor clock speed
- Memory capacity
- Memory type
- Memory clock speed
- The interface used

Video Card Specifications

We will concentrate here on gaming cards. Workstation cards are really a different entity as they are designed specifically for business applications.

Quadro workstation video card from Nvidia

Don't forget

Workstation video cards can cost $3000 and more. The level of performance they provide, and features such as massive resolutions, will never be needed by the home user.

109

When shopping for a video card, you need to consider the following specifications:

Processor Clock Speed
This is often referred to as the Core Clock Speed in the specifications and relates to the speed at which the Global Processing Unit (GPU) runs. As with a CPU, the faster it is, the faster the speed and the better the performance of the card.

Low-end video cards have a GPU running at about 550 MHz, mid-range cards at 700 MHz, and the latest top-end cards up to 950 MHz.

Memory Capacity
A video card's memory capacity is sometimes referred to as the Frame Buffer in the specifications. A common misconception is that the more memory a video card has, the faster it will run. However, memory capacity has absolutely no effect in this regard. What it does do is enable high resolutions, and video quality to be set at high levels.

If the application being run does not need a high quantity of memory, an otherwise identical card with 1 GB of memory will perform just as well as one with 2 GB.

Top-end video cards currently have 2 GB of memory, mid-range cards have 1 GB and low-end cards have 512 MB.

Memory Type
Virtually all video cards currently on the market use a type of DDR memory known as Graphics Double Data Rate (GDDR). This is a derivative of the standard DDR memory used for PCs, which has been optimized for use with video. This memory is available in various versions ranging from GDDR1 to GDDR5.

GDDR1 and 2 are now obsolete but there are still many video cards on the market using GDDR3 and 4. Recent high-end cards all use GDDR5.

Given that GDDR5 offers major improvements over GDDR4, this is the memory standard to go for.

Memory Speed
In the same way that high-speed system memory increases the speed and performance of a computer, high-speed video memory does the same for video cards.

Low-end cards come in at around 800 MHz, mid-range cards at 2 GHz and the latest high-end cards at up to 5 GHz.

Interfaces
There are two separate interfaces to be considered with regard to video cards. The first is built-in and provides an internal link between the video card's processor (GPU) and its memory. It refers to how much data, in bits, can be read from, and written to, the memory in one clock cycle.

High-end cards have a memory interface of 512 bits, mid-range cards have an interface of 256 bits, and low-end cards have a 128 bit interface.

The second is the card's physical interface. Due to the high amounts of data involved with video, video cards need a dedicated high-bandwith bus, and the one currently in use is the PCI-Express 2.1 x16 bus.

Hot tip

Don't confuse the GDDR memory used by video cards with the DDR memory used by computer systems. They are not the same.

This has a data throughput rate of 500 MBps, and while this figure may not seem particularly impressive it is important to realise that the PCI-Express x16 interface provides 32 data channels (two for each of the 16 lanes). As the data throughput figure mentioned above applies to each channel, PCI-Express 2.1 x16 (the latest version) has a total data throughput of 16 GB per second (500 MBps x 32).

Nothing stands still in the world of computer hardware though, and PCI-Express 3.0 x16, which will have a data throughput rate of 1 GBps per channel, plus some other major improvements, is soon to be released.

This raises the question "Should I wait until version 3.0 is available before building my new system?". For the vast majority of users the answer to this has to be no as there is no current software that fully utilizes the capabilities of version 2.1, never mind version 3.0.

Finally, a note about the old AGP video card interface. While it is now out-dated technology, there are still video cards on the market that use it. Don't make the mistake of buying one of these – PCI-Express 2.1 x16 is what you want.

Hot tip

The PCI-Express interface provides sockets of various sizes – x1, x2, x4, and x16. PCI-Express video cards use the x16 socket.

111

Other Factors to Consider

Ports
Video cards come with a range of input and output ports, the quantity and type of which depend on the quality of the card and, also, how modern it is.

Older cards will have a VGA port and possibly a VIVO (also known as TV-Out) port.

More recent cards will have a DVI port, probably a VGA port and maybe a VIVO port.

Higher-end cards often come with two DVI ports. Modern high-end video cards will have two DVI ports, a HDMI (High-Definition) port, and the new DisplayPort.

...cont'd

Above, we see a typical video card output panel with a white DVI port, a blue VGA port and a black VIVO port.

Below, we have a modern high-end video card with two DVI ports on the right, a HDMI port in the middle and a DisplayPort on the left.

Digital Video Interface (DVI)

The DVI port is designed for use with LCD monitors, which need a digital signal.

Video-in/Video-out (VIVO)

The VIVO (video in/video out) port enables you to hook up the PC to other video devices such as a television set. More recent video cards now provide a HDMI port for this purpose.

Video Graphics Array (VGA)

The blue VGA port was designed for use with old CRT monitors. However, it can be used with LCD monitors as well.

High Definition Multimedia Interface (HDMI)

Used to connect video equipment, such as TVs and video recorders, to the PC. It replaces the older VIVO port.

DisplayPort

DisplayPort is a new display interface designed to replace digital (DVI) and analog (VGA) ports in computer monitors and video cards. Currently only found on the latest cards.

Don't forget

If you have a spare monitor, consider getting a video card with dual outputs. This will enable you to run both monitors at the same time, which can be very useful in certain situations.

Dimensions

Many of the top-end video cards are serious pieces of circuitry and by this we don't just mean specifications, we mean big, as in take up a lot of room. This is further compounded by the serious cooling systems these cards require.

Beware

If you go for one of the latest video cards, make sure it will leave room for the other devices you intend to install. Some of these cards come with quite monstrous cooling systems that will occupy an inordinate amount of space in the case.

While you will have no trouble fitting even the largest video card into a full size tower case, with anything smaller you may struggle to accommodate one. So if you are planning on incorporating a high-end video card into your system, make sure that the card will fit.

Note that many gaming cases are designed to eliminate this issue; the Antec Nine Hundred case being a good example. This case allows the drive cages to be relocated to different positions thus creating room for a bulky video card if necessary.

Application Programming Interfaces (APIs)

APIs are basically a set of routines that programmers use to ensure that their software is supported by as wide a range of hardware setups as possible. In relation to video, they allow multimedia applications to utilize hardware acceleration features provided by video systems.

For the API, and thus the application, to work, it must be supported by the PC's video system.

...cont'd

Hot tip

Microsoft release updated versions of DirectX periodically. You can find out what the latest version is (and download it) by going to www.microsoft.com.

There are various APIs, such as OpenGL and Microsoft's Direct X. The latter is the one most commonly used, so you should ensure that your video card supports the latest version of it (currently version 11).

Power and Heat Issues

Power and heat are only issues if you are buying at the top end of the video card market.

The more features packed into a video card, the more power required to run it. You need to consider this when upgrading a video card as it may also be necessary to upgrade the power supply unit. You may, for example, find that you need a 500 watt PSU instead of a 400 watt version – the extra 100 watts to cover the power requirement of the card.

Furthermore, all this power generates lots of heat. While the card's cooling system will keep the card itself cool, this heat will raise the temperature in the system case, and because of this, you may need to install extra fans or invest in a more efficient cooling system.

Noise

There's no getting away from the fact that high-end video cards can be rather intrusive in terms of the noise their cooling fans make.

However, there are ways to reduce, or even eliminate, this. For example, noisy fans can be replaced with silent versions, sound proofing kits can reduce noise levels considerably; while opting for a water-cooled system or a high-end fanless heatsink, does away with the need for fans completely.

Bundled Extras

Many video cards come with "extras" that can help to soften the impact on your wallet. The most typical example is the inclusion of one or two PC games.

There may also be some video-related software on the installation disk, e.g. video-editing.

Hot tip

Most video cards include a couple of games in the box. While they are never the latest, some of them are fairly recent. If you are torn between two cards, the games on offer might be the deciding factor.

Video Capture Devices

Video, in all its various forms (viewing, recording, editing, etc) is one of the most popular applications with PC users. One of the first questions people new to this ask is "How do I get the video into my PC?".

The answer is with the aid of a video capture card. There are several types of this device and each have their pros and cons. The following will help you to decide which one is best for your purposes.

TV Tuners

As the name might suggest, these devices are concerned primarily with allowing you to watch television on your PC, either full-screen or in a resizable window.

Available as either expansion cards or USB external models, they can display video from a variety of sources. These include standard TV antennas, cable networks, DVD players, camcorders and video recorders.

However, these devices can also be used to record TV (using the PC's hard drive as the recording medium), and to capture video from other types of video device.

TV tuners do have their limitations, however. Very few of them provide a TV-out facility, which other types of capture card do. Also, recording formats offered can be limited; often only MPEG-2, which does not provide high-quality video.

That said, if your requirements in terms of video quality and features are not particularly high, these devices are adequate. For watching TV, they are fine. If you intend to do a lot of video work though, or require high-quality output, a specialized video capture card will be a better option.

Hot tip

Anyone buying a TV tuner with the intention of watching a lot of TV on the PC should choose a model that includes a remote control. Otherwise, you will have to get up and use the mouse or keyboard every time you want to switch channels or adjust the volume.

...cont'd

Video Cards

Some video cards provide video capturing facilities; many however, don't. Also, there are some that require a driver download from the manufacturer's website to enable this function. Therefore, this is an issue that needs to be checked prior to purchase.

Even with cards that do, however, remember that video cards are designed with one specific purpose in mind; anything else they offer is of lesser importance, and thus may also be of lesser quality.

Another problem is that video cards simply do not have enough room on the back plate to accommodate the full range of sockets necessary to connect all the various types of video device.

Video Capture Cards

For those who are serious about working with video, a dedicated capture card is by far the best option. These devices are also available as external models (shown below) that connect to the system via a USB or FireWire port.

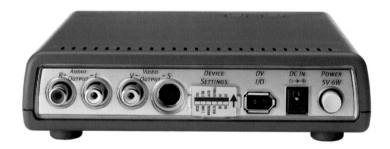

Apart from the higher level of overall quality provided, you will also get much more in the way of connectivity options, such as Mic, Line out, Composite Video Input, S-Video, HDMI, and 4- and 6-pin 1394 (FireWire) sockets.

Other advantages include:

- A higher range of input and output formats

- Faster data transfer rates

- Higher capture resolutions and color depth capabilities

- The ability to export video as well as import it

Beware

Associated sound can be an issue when using a video card to import video. Many of them do not have native support for sound and rely on the PC's sound system to do the job. With this type of setup, getting the sound to synchronize with the video can be problematic.

PC Entertainment Centers

If your reason for upgrading is general entertainment rather than something specific, such as gaming or running graphics applications, you can really push the boat out and go for a PC entertainment center. These come in two types: a) a purpose built unit, and b) a collection of home entertainment devices connected to, and controlled by, a PC. Both provide the following:

- TV

- Video

- Audio

- Digital video recording (using the hard drive as the medium)

- Standard PC functions

Hot tip

Purpose built entertainment centers are expensive. However, they do combine the various devices into one unit, all of which can be controlled with one remote control.

The advantage of a purpose built unit is that with the exception of the speakers and the TV, everything is housed in one compact unit. Not only is this a real space-saver; aesthetically, it looks much better – PCs are not the most attractive things to have in your living room.

They do have drawbacks, though. First, buying one of these is more than a simple upgrade – they are not cheap.

Second, being essentially a PC that requires cooling and hence a fan, they make more noise than might be acceptable in a communal room.

Building one yourself is a much cheaper option as you already have the PC and probably the other devices as well. All you need is a video capture device with the necessary inputs/outputs and you're in business.

The disadvantage is that the PC will usually have to be moved into the living room so that your TV, music system and video players can be connected to it. However, if you are prepared to run extra cabling, your entertainment devices can be connected to a PC in a different room.

A better option is to build a wireless home network. In conjunction with a portable PC, such as a laptop, you will be able to control the system from any location in the house.

Installing a Video Card

The example below demonstrates the installation of a PCI-Express x16 video card.

1 Locate the colored PCI-Express x16 socket

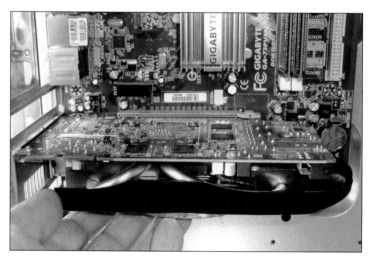

2 Slide the card into the socket. When it is fully inserted the retaining clip will automatically lock it in place

3   Screw the backplate to the case chassis

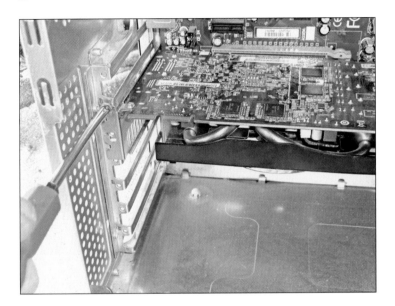

4   If the card requires a dedicated power supply, connect the 4- or 6-pin PCI-Express power connector from the PSU

Don't forget

Low-end video cards may not require a separate power supply; high-end cards will. If yours does, don't forget to connect it, otherwise you will have no video.

Computer Sound Systems

Integrated Sound

Virtually all motherboards provide an in-built sound system and the ones supplied with motherboards built in the last four or five years or so are actually very good, offering features such as support for multiple-speaker setups, DirectX, EAX and DirectSound 3D.

However, they do have three inherent disadvantages.

1) They are prone to picking up electrical interference from other motherboard components. This results in a low signal-to-noise ratio, which manifests itself as pops, clicks and buzzes in the output signal

2) Due to space restrictions on the motherboard's input/output panel, they do not provide the full range of sockets

3) Integrated systems do make a hit on overall system performance as they rely on the CPU to do all the number-crunching. While the effects are negligible, they are, nevertheless, there

Accordingly, integrated systems are not suitable for the following applications:

● High-quality sound reproduction

● Music mastering

● Hardcore gaming

Users with an interest in any of these will need to install a separate sound card. A possible exception is gaming, depending on the degree of sophistication required (see margin note).

However, for all other purposes, an integrated sound system will be perfectly adequate.

With regard to upgrading an old integrated system to a more recent one that offers better quality and more features, this really doesn't make any sense as it will mean replacing the motherboard. A much easier (and cheaper) option, would be to simply install a sound card. A mid-range, or maybe even a budget model, should do nicely.

Beware

As with video, integrated sound systems do have a slightly adverse effect on system performance. Those of you upgrading with the intention of increasing the speed of the PC should be aware of this.

Beware

The main sound requirement for gamers is 3D surround-sound, which requires 3D and speaker connection support. While current integrated systems provide both of these, the quality of 3D sound they offer is not as realistic as that offered by dedicated sound cards. The bottom line here is that if you want the best quality surround-sound, you will need a sound card. Otherwise, a recent integrated system will be adequate.

Sound Cards

Sound cards are available with a range of specialized features and options, and if you're not careful, you could end up buying one that is not ideal for the task in hand.

Games and DVD Movies

For those of you who are seeking to enhance your game-playing or DVD movie experience in terms of sound, the quality of a sound card's output is of less importance than its ability to create the illusion that you are in the middle of the action literally. For example, if a game character walks behind you, his footsteps should sound as though they are coming from over your shoulder.

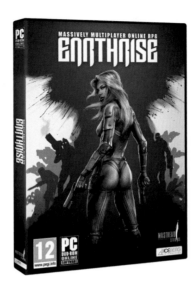

To be able to do this, the sound card must provide the following:

- Multiple-speaker support – each pair of speakers requires a line-out socket. So a five- or six-speaker system will require three of these, and a seven- or eight six-speaker system will require four

- 3D sound – also known as Positional Audio, this technology accurately recreates the relative positioning of sound in a three-dimensional environment. The de facto standard is currently Creative's EAX

For gamers, Direct X is important and the card should support the version used by the games.

Also important is the number of simultaneous sounds the card can process (these are referred to as channels in the specifications). If the application throws more of these at the sound card than it is designed to handle, the system's CPU has to help out, which makes a hit on overall system performance. The game's frame rate may also be adversely affected. 32 channels is a reasonable starting point; anything higher is good.

Beware

Gamers need to be aware that some low-end sound cards actually use the computer's CPU to do the processing. With systems running a low-end CPU, this can result in a lower frame-rate that reduces the "smoothness" of gameplay. Integrated sound systems, no matter how highly specified, tend to cause the same problem.

Hot tip

The term "channels" is also used to describe the number of speakers that can be connected to a sound card. For example, a three-channel card can support six speakers: two for each channel.

...cont'd

Music Systems

With the addition of a high-quality sound card and speakers, a

PC can be turned into an audio system every bit as good as a purpose-built unit. Furthermore, it will offer many more options, such as editing, disc writing, and storage facilities.

Although it may be desirable in such a system, 3D sound will be less important than the fidelity (purity) of the sound card's output. This is determined by the following specifications:

- Bit-Depth – this describes how much of the original sound file is reproduced by the card. High bit-depth means high-fidelity and dynamic range. CDs use a bit-depth of 16, so if your music collection is stored on this type of media, you need a 16-bit sound card. DVD and Blu-ray discs use a bit-depth of 24

- Sampling Rate – this determines the range of frequencies that can be converted to digital format by the sound card, and thus the accuracy of the reproduction. A good card will offer a sampling rate of at least 48 KHz

- Signal-To-Noise Ratio – this is a measure of how "clean" a sound signal is. The higher the amount of background noise (electrical interference, etc), the lower the signal-to-noise ratio. Low-end sound cards will have an SNR of some 75 decibels, while top-end cards will offer 100 decibels

- Total Harmonic Distortion – this is a measurement of the noise produced by the sound card itself during the process of converting the analog signal to a digital signal. A good quality card will have a THD of no more than 0.01%

Hot tip

The most important specifications are bit-depth, which relates to the amount of data reproduced, and the signal-to-noise ratio, which relates to the amount of background noise (hiss).

One problem inherent in all computers that can spoil an otherwise high-quality sound signal is electrical interference from other components. There are two ways to minimize this:

1) Isolate the sound card as far as possible (see page 124)

2) Buy a sound card that comes with a break-out box as shown below

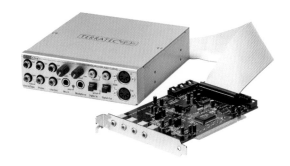

This unit either fits into a spare drive bay or sits on the desktop. It eliminates electrical interference by converting the analog signal to digital form before it is sent to the card in the PC.

Hot tip

Sound cards that come with a break-out box provide higher signal-to-noise ratios than those that don't. This is important for those who require as clean a signal as possible.

Music Creation

Sound cards for musicians are the most complex of all. Not only must they provide a high-quality signal, they must also offer music mastering features, such as preamplifiers, synthesizers and wave-mixers.

These cards almost always come with a break-out box as described above. Not only does this eliminate the issue of noise, the box also provides the full range of input/output sockets. These include balanced analog inputs/outputs, digital inputs/outputs in S/PDIF, FireWire, HDMI, MIDI, and a Phono (stereo) input. These cover virtually all types of device.

Hot tip

S/PDIF and HDMI connections are used for transferring digital data, and are found on most consumer video equipment. A sound card that includes these connections will enable users to hook-up their PCs to these devices.

Installing a Sound Card

We have already mentioned that sound cards are prone to picking up electrical interference from other system components. For this reason, you should install the card in the slot furthest from the other cards, i.e. right at the bottom, as shown on the right.

Insert the card in the socket furthest away from the other devices. This is to minimize electrical interference

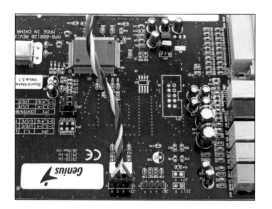

Connect the audio cable from the CD/DVD drive (if necessary)

Screw the card's backplate to the case chassis

Speaker Systems

A good set of speakers is an essential part of a high-quality sound system. You may have the best sound card in the galaxy but if it is connected to a cheap speaker system, you will get poor sound.

PC speakers are available either as a pair (as supplied by most PC manufacturers) or as a multiple-speaker system. The type of setup you go for depends on the intended use.

Music buffs who simply want high-fidelity will be best served by a pair of high-quality stereo speakers – a surround-sound system is not necessary.

Gamers and movie fans who want surround-sound will need a multiple-speaker system, as shown below. When buying one of these, don't forget to check that your sound system is capable of fully utilizing it. There's no point in buying a 7:1 speaker system if you have only three line-out jacks.

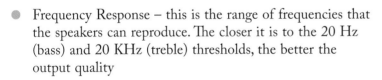

Whichever type of setup you go for, considering the following specifications will ensure that your chosen speakers are up to scratch.

- Frequency Response – this is the range of frequencies that the speakers can reproduce. The closer it is to the 20 Hz (bass) and 20 KHz (treble) thresholds, the better the output quality

- Sensitivity – this is sometimes referred to as Sound Pressure Level and indicates the efficiency with which the speakers convert power to sound. Look for a figure of at least 90 decibels

- Wattage – while this is not an indication of quality, it is a fact that speakers with a high wattage rating do generally produce better sound

125

Hot tip

Surround-Sound speaker systems range from 2:1 (one large subwoofer for bass reproduction, and two smaller satellites – one for mid-range and one for treble reproduction) up to 8:1 (one sub-woofer and seven satellites).

Hot tip

Speaker wattage is rated in two ways: peak power and continuous power. The manufacturers like to emphasize the former as this is the higher of the two figures. However, buyers should be more concerned with the continuous (RMS) power rating as this gives a more accurate indication of the speaker's capabilities.

Speaker Connection

Connecting PC speakers is simply a matter of plugging them into the sound system's output jacks. To make it easy, most current sound cards and speakers use color-coded connections.

Hot tip

If your sound card or speaker connections are not color-coded for easy identification, refer to the documentation.

Front speakers plug into the green, rear speakers into the black, and center and side speakers into the orange sockets.

Positioning Speakers

To get the best effect out of surround-sound systems, the speakers must be optimally placed. While there is a large degree of personal preference involved here, the following illustration of a 7:1 speaker system setup is a good guideline.

Hot tip

Correct speaker positioning is particularly important in 3D games. In a violent fast-paced 3D world, when a sound is supposed to come from your right-rear flank but seems to come from directly behind you, it could cost you a virtual life.

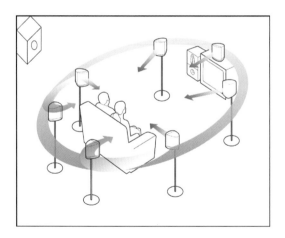

Firstly, the sub-woofer: this is not critical as bass is non-directional. However, the best results will be obtained from placing it next to a wall or in a corner.

The center speaker should be placed on top of the monitor or TV, and the front-right and front-left speakers to either side and angled towards the listener.

Two speakers should be placed on either side and the final two at the rear.

8 A Reliable PC

This chapter focuses on the causes of an unreliable system and the upgrades that can be made in order to resolve these issues.

What Makes a PC Unreliable?

An unreliable PC is one that behaves erratically, does things that it shouldn't do and doesn't do things that it should. Typical symptoms are frequent crashing, locking-up and sudden system reboots, all of which are common causes of data loss. Actions of this type can also result in other problems, such as corruption of the operating system.

Unreliability is caused by either a low-quality, faulty or over-extended item of hardware, or problems with the operating system or a software program. Hardware is the most likely culprit, so we'll look at this first.

The PC's Power Supply

A computer has two different power supplies: the AC input from the wall socket and the DC output from the power supply unit. Both can be the source of problems that make a PC unreliable.

Power Supply Unit (PSU)

These devices are prone to two types of problem and, in each case, the cause is bad design and the use of low-quality components; in other words, they are cheap and nasty. Unfortunately, this happens to describe the majority of PSUs supplied by PC manufacturers as part of their systems.

The first problem is that the current they supply tends to fluctuate. This means that the PC is sometimes not getting enough and at other times it is getting too much. If these variations in current exceed the tolerances to which the PC's components are built, it behaves erratically.

The second problem is that they fail (being highly stressed components, this is inevitable), and when they do, they do it in a big way – a loud bang, accompanied by a puff of smoke. The result is a surge of current though the system that can, and does, destroy other components. Typically, these are the CPU and memory, and sometimes the hard drive as well (where all your data is kept).

So those of you who need or want a reliable system must make sure that your current PSU is not one of these low-end affairs, and in most cases this will mean upgrading it.

Hot tip

Even if they're OK to begin with, low-end PSUs are much more likely to develop the type of faults that affect a PC's stability.

Beware

PSUs are a part of a computer system that most people never consider; they are much more interested in the CPU speed, the video card and the amount of memory. PC manufacturers are aware of this and use cheap PSUs to cut the cost of their systems.

There are, of course, other reasons to upgrade the PSU and these include:

● To supply the extra power requirements of new devices that the existing PSU is incapable of delivering

● To provide the power connections required by devices using new technology, e.g. the PCI-Express interface

● To reduce the noise levels of the PC by taking advantage of "silent" PSUs

Whatever your reason for upgrading the PSU, considering the following factors will ensure you buy the right one.

Protection Circuitry

A good quality PSU incorporates circuits that monitor variables such as temperature and current, and if any of them exceed designated limits the PSU simply shuts down (rather than blowing, as cheap models do). This will, of course, also shut down the PC but no damage is done to its components. Low-end PSUs do not have this feature.

These circuits also offer some protection against fluctuations in the external AC supply, which can be another source of problems.

Cooling

Cheaper PSUs, as supplied by PC manufacturers, will have one cooling fan, which is adequate for normal operating conditions. Better quality PSUs, however, usually have an extra fan, mounted underneath or to the side, which will kick-in when the PSU is highly loaded. This provides extra cooling when it is really needed and can extend the working life of the PSU considerably.

Connectors

The PSU must supply the type of connectors used by the components in your system and, also, enough of them.

For many years, ATA hard drives and CD/DVD drives were powered by a 4-pin molex connector. Modern drives, however, now use the SATA interface, which has a different type of connector. Not all modern PSUs provide these molex connectors so if your system still has an ATA drive, make sure the PSU you buy does provide them.

Hot tip

How do you know if you have a low-quality PSU? Easy – check its specifications to see if it incorporates protection circuitry. If it doesn't, you should replace it.

Hot tip

Another specification to take note of is the PSU's efficiency rating. This is the ratio of the amount of power that goes into the PSU compared to the amount that goes out. Efficiency is expressed as a percentage and a good figure to aim at is 65 % - 85 %.

...cont'd

As an alternative, you can buy a SATA to Molex converter.

If you are adding, or upgrading, a PCI-Express video card be aware that these devices require a dedicated power supply in the form of a 4- or 6-pin connector. Make sure your new PSU provides one.

Power Rating

The power supply unit must be capable of providing the power requirements of every component in the system with a bit to spare. The latter is important for two reasons:

1) The PSU (as with any device) will not last very long if it is run continuously at full load

2) Having some spare power capacity will allow you to add extra devices at a later date without having to also buy a PSU with a higher power rating

The table below shows you the approximate maximum power requirements of all the components in a computer system, and this will enable you to calculate the amount of power required by your system.

130

Component	Power Required
Low- to mid-range video card	150 W
High-end video card	250 W
Expansion cards	5 W
ATA hard drive	15 W
SATA hard drive	10 W
SCSI hard drive	40 W
Optical drives	25 W
Floppy drives	5 W
Cooling fans	2.5 W
Motherboard	35 W
1 GB DDR memory	5 W
High-end CPUs	130 W
Low-end CPUs	45 W
LEDs	1 W

External Power Supply

The AC supply is another factor that affects the stability of a PC. External power supplies are subject to a range of faults: these include power surges, line noise and frequency variation all of which can adversely affect the stability of a computer.

Power surges are one of the most common and have a similar effect on a PC as a low-quality PSU. They also stress components and, over time, have a cumulative effect that can result in them failing well before they should.

While there is nothing that you can do about the quality of the signal, there are three levels of protection that you can employ:

1) Install a good quality PSU that has protection circuitry. This usually offers some protection against AC faults as well

2) Fit a power surge suppressor (shown below). These devices "smooth" out momentary increases in the AC signal, thus ensuring the supply to the PC is at a constant level

Courtesy of Belkin Corporation

3) Fit a Line Conditioner. These are a step up from surge suppressors and not only eliminate power surges, but also eliminate electrical interference that causes line noise

For home PC use, a top-end PSU and a power surge suppressor will ensure both a "clean" AC input to the PC, and protection against damage to other system components in the event of problems with the PSU.

Hot tip

Those of you who do mission-critical work on your PC might consider an Uninterruptible Power Supply Unit (UPS). These units provide a battery powered backup that takes over when the AC supply has failed. Typically, they will supply several hours of power.

Heat

Another factor that the upgrader needs to be aware of is that of heat and the effect that an excess amount of it will have on the computer's components. First, it stresses them beyond their design tolerances and, second it makes them operate in an erratic fashion. The former causes damage and the latter causes unreliability.

Excess heat is likely to be an issue only when power-hungry devices are added to the system; the most typical example being one of the latest video cards. These devices generate serious amounts of heat and while they all come equipped with cooling systems that directs most of it away from the device, inevitably much of it remains in the system case. The same applies to high-end CPUs.

Cramming a lot of devices (power-hungry or not) into the case can have the same effect. For example, you may have two hard drives, a DVD drive, a video card, a TV tuner card, a sound card, a modem, and an SCSI or FireWire card.

In either of these situations, it may be necessary to install another cooling fan. Virtually all system cases have mounting points for these, which are usually located at the rear and the top.

Alternatively, in the case of a high-end video card, you can fit a dedicated fan (shown below). This device plugs into the expansion slot next to the video card where it is ideally situated to keep it cool.

Overheating can also be caused, or compounded, by dust blocking the out-take vents of both the PSU and the system case. A can of compressed air or a good healthy puff will clear this away. Don't forget to do the circuit boards as well; these will be covered by a layer of dust which, in case you didn't know, is an insulator.

Replacing a Power Supply Unit

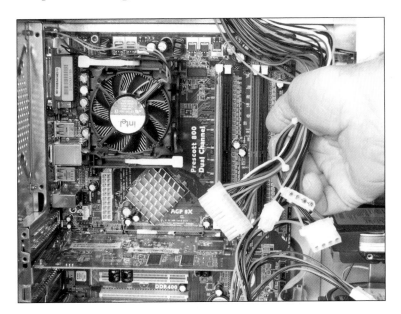

1 Disconnect the existing PSU's cables

2 Unscrew the PSU (at the top rear of the system case)

3 Remove the PSU from the case

4 Install the new PSU by reversing steps 1 to 3

Software

There are two types of software that are well known for rendering a computer system unstable and, hence, unreliable. The first is hardware drivers and the second is malware.

Hardware Drivers

A driver is a small program that acts as an interface between hardware and the operating system. Essentially, it's a set of instructions that tells the operating system how to control and communicate with the associated hardware device. In many cases, it also allows the user to make configuration changes to the device. For example, a printer driver lets you set the print quality, amongst many other things.

One of the problems with drivers is that they often contain bugs (errors), which can cause incompatibility issues with other hardware devices. This can have a knock-on effect that may result in system-wide problems, one of which is general instability.

To resolve this, hardware manufacturers periodically release updated drivers for their products in which the bugs have been fixed. So downloading and installing updated drivers for all your devices as and when they are released will minimize this cause of problems.

Malware

This term is used to describe the multitude of pesky programs that sneak themselves on to a user's PC when certain websites are visited, or are hidden in seemingly legitimate programs. These include spyware, which sends details of the user's PC back to the maker, adware, which opens advertising pop-up windows in the user's browser, and hijackers, which take over the user's browser and redirect all searches to specific sites.

Apart from being extremely irritating, these programs can have a seriously adverse effect on the performance and reliability of the PC. While it is possible to remove them, prevention is much easier than the cure. To this end, invest in a good anti-virus program such as Norton Internet Security. This program (and others of its ilk) also protect against malware.

Also, do not install freeware and shareware programs downloaded from the Internet (see margin note).

Hot tip

The first thing an upgrader should do having installed a new hardware device, is go to the manufacturer's website and download the latest driver for the device.

Beware

Those of you who download free and shareware applications should be aware that in many cases the program will have an unwelcome attachment. Software, music and movie files obtained via the file-sharing networks are another source of these programs. It is essential that you scan downloads of this type with both anti-virus and malware removal programs.

9 Improve Your Input Options

Input devices include the mouse, keyboard and game controllers. These devices come in a range of models designed for different applications.

The Mouse

Computer users today have an enormous range of mice to choose from. They come in different colors, shapes, sizes, and offer features and technologies that make their predecessor, the ball and wheel mouse, seem positively prehistoric.

Currently, the most common type is the optical mouse. These work by using a Light Emitting Device (LED) to bounce light off the work surface. The reflected light is processed, and if any changes are detected, the new coordinates are passed to the computer.

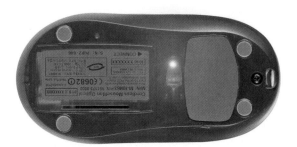

LED sensor on the underside of the mouse

The result is extremely smooth operation and a good degree of accuracy. Furthermore, as they contain no moving parts, they are extremely reliable and require no maintenance. For every-day PC use, they are more than adequate.

So why would anyone want to upgrade to something better? Well, one reason is aesthetics – the days of bland beige colored mice are long gone. Todays mice are visually appealing; so much so that many are bought purely on this basis.

A more practical reason is ergonomics. Millions of people all over the world spend a considerable part of their day with a mouse in their hand, and so one that it as easy as possible to use is a definite boon.

Beware

Cordless mice can get through a lot of batteries over a period of months. For this reason, look for a model that comes with rechargeable batteries and a charging unit.

This is where cordless mice come into their own as the lack of a cord is one less obstacle to work around. This enables the user to sit further away from the monitor as well. Shape, size and weight are also considerations with regard to comfort and, hence, productivity. Some high-end mice come with an adjustable weight cartridge that enables the user to customize the device's weight.

Some people cannot use a standard mouse due to disabilities. Trackballs, which are basically an upended ball and wheel mouse, and can be operated with a single finger and require no wrist movement offer an alternative way of controlling the cursor.

A further advantage is that they can be used on any surface as the ball doesn't come into contact with it.

Hot tip

Laser mice can be used on a much greater range of surfaces than standard optical mice.

The most compelling reason to upgrade a mouse however, is that of precision. Standard optical mice are accurate enough for most purposes but there are applications that require more from the mouse than they can deliver.

Graphics programs and PC gaming are two typical examples. Anyone who has used a standard optical mouse with these types of application will immediately notice the difference if they switch to a laser mouse (shown left).

137

These devices offer a tracking precision that is some three times greater than that of an optical mouse. Furthermore, this can be changed at the click of a button to suit the task at hand.

Don't forget

For applications that require a high degree of precision, laser mice are the way to go.

Laser mice also have a higher degree of sensitivity, which means the cursor can be moved further with less movement of the mouse.

Another advantage that many offer is built-in memory that enables the user to set up a number of profiles (dpi and tracking settings, macros, and LED colors) so that the ideal configuration for various applications can be selected with the click of a button.

Keyboards

For general purpose use, keyboards supplied by PC manufacturers get the job done. However, they don't look anything special, their key action is not the nicest, and they have limited functionality. If you are using one of these to do serious amounts of typing, upgrading to a high-quality model is highly recommended.

One of the things you'll notice is how much more positive and responsive the action of the keys is. This is due to the fact that good keyboards use a mechanical key system as opposed to the membrane system used by their lesser siblings. Each key is assigned its own switch, which makes an audible click when depressed. When it is released, it springs back into place quickly.

In a membrane keyboard, all the keys sit on a sheet of plastic. This is imprinted with a metallic pattern that, when touched by a key, acts like the switch in a mechanical keyboard and sends the "key depressed" signal to the computer. This is why these keyboards have a spongy feel to them. It is also why they are much cheaper as they have many less parts inside them.

Also available for serious typists are ergonomically designed keyboards. These are constructed in a way that allows users to hold their hands in a more comfortable, slightly angled position, while typing. This type of keyboard can also help prevent, or alleviate, Carpal Tunnel Syndrome. This is an affliction that affects the wrists.

Taking this concept a bit further are split keyboards that have an adjustable hinge in the middle to vary the angle at which the keys are presented to the user's hands.

Quality and ergonomics are not the only reasons to upgrade a keyboard; many of these devices are tailored to meet specific user requirements. For example, those of you who frequently use Microsoft office applications can buy models that have keys relevant to Word, PowerPoint, Excel, etc. Others have keys that control multimedia functions such as play and pause, and Internet and email functions.

This keyboard from Viewsonic has keys for office, multimedia, Internet, and email applications

Game Controllers

Anyone thinking of getting into PC gaming in a serious way will find that the features, and levels of precision, offered by standard keyboards and mice just don't cut the mustard. They have four better options available to them:

Gaming Keyboards

For some game genres, keyboards are the best type of controller. An example is strategy games, such as Microsoft's Age of Empires, where most of the action is controlled by the keyboard.

While standard keyboards are adequate, much better results will be had from one of the specialized gaming keyboards. These have a multitude of programmable keys that allow the user to customize it to suit specific games.

Most also have an integral joystick, plus illuminated keys that allow games to be played in the dark (hardly essential, but cool nevertheless).

One of the most important features that they offer to gamers is the ability to set up macro commands that combine multiple keystrokes into one. For example, with a standard keyboard, getting a game character to jump forward and kick-out simultaneously will require three keys to be pressed at the same time. A gaming keyboard will do this with one keystroke.

Hot tip

The gaming keyboard (shown right) provides a backlit, adjustable LCD that shows you useful system information during gameplay.

Another type of gaming keyboard consists of a base unit on which can be placed customized keysets designed for use with specific games. If this interests you, visit Steelseries at www.steelseries.com.

Joysticks

Joysticks are designed for use with flight simulators, although they can also be used with other genres. An important consideration

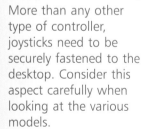

Hot tip

More than any other type of controller, joysticks need to be securely fastened to the desktop. Consider this aspect carefully when looking at the various models.

with these devices is weight and build quality; joysticks are subjected to a lot of abuse and need to be up to the job physically. Another is how securely they fix to the desktop; a joystick that hops around is not going to be of much use.

Another important feature to look for is a twist handle; this gives you rudder control in a flight game.

A good joystick will also have several programmable buttons that allow configurations to be set up for various games using the associated software.

Steering Wheels

Steering wheels are designed specifically for racing games such as Formula One and Nascar.

One of the most important features these devices should provide is force feedback. While this is also available with other types of controller, it is particularly effective in driving games as it lets you "feel" every bump and crash.

For those playing Formula 1 games, the device should provide gear "shifter" switches in the form of paddles (this is how gears are changed in current F1 cars).

Also, check that foot pedals are included in the package (not all do) to provide a truly authentic racing experience. A secure clamping system is essential.

Hot tip

Force feedback technology creates the sense of touch and no decent controller these days would be complete without it.

GamePads

These devices are basically a cross between a wheel and a joystick as they provide features common to both but without the high level of precision. This makes them ideal for use by those who play various types of game.

Any good gamepad will provide at least eight programmable buttons, two analog joysticks (also known as thumbsticks), and a four-way D pad (used for navigation purposes). Top-end gamepads will have an eight-way D pad for more precise control.

Another consideration is the length of the cord. This should be at least six feet to give you room in which to maneuver.

Hot tip

Game controllers are available in cordless versions that allow the user to sit a lot further back from the monitor. It is a particularly useful feature with gamepads, as a cord flapping about can be restrictive.

Scanners

Scanners are devices that are used to import an image of a picture or document into the user's PC. The difference between low- and high-end models is the speed at which they do it, the quality of the image produced and the level of control offered.

When upgrading this device, or buying one for the first time, you need to consider the following specifications.

Scan Resolution

This is a measure of how much detail is reproduced by the scan process and is expressed in dots per inch (dpi). The higher this figure, the better the quality of the scanned image. The majority of scanners have a maximum dpi of 600 and for most purposes, this is more than enough. The only type of application that requires a much higher scan resolution is image enlarging and for this a high-end model may be needed.

The following table shows what level of resolution is required by the most common applications.

Don't forget

Unless your images are going to be enlarged, the highest scan resolution that you will need is 600 dpi.

Application	Resolution
Images for commercial printing	300 dpi
Images to be enlarged	1200 dpi upwards
Photos for printing on inkjet printers	300 dpi
Text documents	300 dpi
Line art (drawings, diagrams, etc)	300 dpi
Images for websites	72 dpi

When looking at a scanner's specifications, you may see two figures for resolution – hardware and interpolated. The hardware figure is the one you want; ignore the interpolated figure (see top margin note).

Specifications

Scanner Type	Flatbed
Image Sensor	CCD
Resolutions, Optical	6,400 dpi (max)
Resolutions, Hardware	6,400 x 9,600 dpi
Resolutions, Interpolated	12,800 x 12,800 dpi
Color Depth	48-bit
Interface	Hi-Speed USB 2.0/1.1

Color Depth

This tells you how many colors the scanner can register and is measured in bits. 24-bits is the minimum required for good color reproduction. However, as virtually all scanners these days can scan at a depth of 48-bits, this isn't really an issue. It's worth checking out though, if you're looking at the low-end of the market.

Optical Density

Also known as Dynamic Range, this indicates how wide a range of tones the scanner can recognize, and is measured on a scale from 0.0 (perfect white) to 4.0 (perfect black).

Most flatbed scanners have an OD around 2.8-3.0 which is fine for photographs. Slides, negatives and transparencies, which have broader tonal ranges, will need a higher OD of about 3.4.

Interface

Currently, most scanners intended for home use employ the USB 2 interface. However, with the recent introduction of USB 3, we recommend anyone intending to upgrade their scanner to get a USB 3 model.

Scanning Area

Most flatbed scanners are large enough to scan at letter size. Larger documents will require a scanner with a correspondingly bigger scanning area (and price).

Beware

Interpolated resolution is basically a software enhancement of the true (hardware) resolution, and is achieved by adding extra pixels to the image. While it can improve image quality to a limited degree, it is nowhere near as good as the quoted figure may suggest. Take this with a very large pinch of salt.

Hot tip

Many scanners offer optional accessories that extend their functionality. These include slide and negative attachments, and sheet-feeders.

Hot tip

Scanners that offer one-touch buttons for common tasks can save you a lot of time.

Web Cameras

Traditionally, the only practical uses for these devices has been video links for conferencing purposes, and for recording video "greeting cards" to send to friends and family.

However, thanks to the current ease and affordability of setting up a home wireless network (see pages 161-162), there is now another way to employ them.

In conjunction with a network and a basic software program, a handful of these devices can be used to create a flexible and low-cost home surveillance system. This can be used for a multitude of purposes, such as detecting intruders and keeping an eye on the baby. It can also be easily extended or relocated; for example, moving a camera outdoors to make sure the guys re-laying the drive are doing the job properly.

Microphones

Microphones are used as a means of getting the spoken word into a PC. Typical uses are dubbing home movies and voice recognition. They can also be used in conjunction with a PC for voice links over the Internet.

The latter (known as Internet Telephony) has been around for a while now, but technical issues that have resulted in poor quality connections and unreliability have prevented it from taking off. However, while still far from perfect, the technology behind it has now improved to the extent that it is now a serious option, particularly for overseas calls.

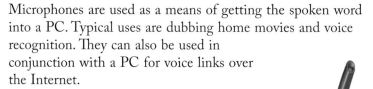

Internet telephony is becoming increasingly popular, particularly for international communications, and all that's required is a PC, a microphone of reasonable quality and a software program.

10 Data Output Options

In this chapter, we look at the two main devices used to present a computer's data – monitors and printers.

Types of LCD Panel

With the demise of CRT monitors, all monitors on the market are now of the active matrix LCD type. However, few people realize that there are several different types of panel used in LCD monitors. Any upgrader looking for a high quality model needs to be aware of this.

Twisted Nematic (TN)

TN panels are cheap to manufacture and have the added bonus of very fast response times (2 to 5 ms).

The main drawback of TN is its color reproduction. As it represents colors using only 6 bits per RGB color, it is unable to display the full 16.7 million colors available in 24-bit true color. TN panels get round this limitation by using a simulating technique called dithering, which is essentially a compromise between quality and cost.

Other issues with TN is that its viewing angles and contrast ratios are the worst of any current LCD panel technology.

Vertical Alignment (VA)

There are several types of VA technology such as S-PVA and MVA, and they all offer better color reproduction than TN panels as they have higher contrast ratios (which results in more accurate black levels). They also offer wider viewing angles.

However, they suffer from two inherent problems: First, their response times are the worst of all the various types of panel and, second, they are afflicted by "color shifting", which is when the image changes, or shifts, when viewed from a slightly different angle, causing uneven brightness levels across the display.

In Plane Switching (IPS)

IPS panels are the best overall LCD technology for image quality, color accuracy and viewing angles (up to 178 degrees). Their only drawback is slightly slower response times than provided by TN panels.

However, this is only likely to be an issue for hardcore gamers who require the fastest possible response times. For all other PC uses and, hence, users, IPS panels are without doubt the best choice.

Which Monitor Do I Need?

With such a vast range of LCD monitors available, it is important that you consider exactly what you need from your monitor before you part with the cash. The following is a guide:

Home Users

For home users it's a trade-off between price and performance. Extra features such as speakers or USB ports should be taken into account and, depending on the PC's location, aesthetics may be an issue as well.

Important features:

- Price
- Clarity, e.g. sharp text
- Aesthetics

Business Users

The important thing for business users is productivity. Extras may be useful but are not as essential as good image quality, and ergonomics for comfortable and extended viewing.

Important Features:

- Large display area
- Ergonomics, e.g. adjustability
- Energy efficiency
- Reliability
- Display quality

Digital Photographers/Graphic Artists

Many monitors are unable to display color accurately and the printer's output will thus be significantly different. This is an important issue for business users working with digital images and so they need high-end LCDs, which offer highly accurate color scales plus color calibration options.

Important Features:

- Color accuracy
- Excellent screen geometry
- Large display area
- High resolution

Hot tip

Some monitors have an anti-reflective screen coating. This helps to reduce glare and ambient light reflection and so provide a brighter, more vivid picture.

Gamers

The primary requirement for gamers is quick response to their key and mouse commands. Image and sound quality is also important but play second fiddle to rapid graphic response.

Important Features:

- Response time
- Color accuracy
- Large display area

Movie Buffs

The requirements for those who watch movies/video on their monitor are similar to those for gamers, plus some.

Important Features:

- Response time
- Color accuracy
- Large display area
- Wide aspect ratio
- Front-panel inputs
- Alternate signal inputs

Monitor Specifications

Specifications to consider are:

Aspect Ratio

The standard aspect ratio for monitors is 4:3, but wide-screen models have one of 16:9 or 16:10. If you intend to watch movies or HDTV in wide-screen format it will be necessary to buy one of these.

Contrast Ratio

A monitor's contrast ratio is the measurement of the difference in light intensity between the brightest (white) and darkest (black) tones. If it is too low, the image will look washed-out, whereas a high contrast ratio will result in a vibrant colorful image.

However, you should be aware that this measurement will vary throughout the screen due to the slight variations in the lighting behind the panel.

Don't forget

For the best quality HD video, your monitor must have a native resolution of 1920 x 1080

148

Manufacturers will use the highest contrast ratio they can find on a screen, so the figure quoted in the specifications can be somewhat deceptive.

Resolution

The monitor's native, or fixed, resolution must be suitable for your applications and so will determine the size of the monitor you buy. 17- and 19-inch monitors have a native resolution of 1280 x 1024, 20- and 21-inch monitors 1600 x 1200, 23-inch monitors 1920 x 1200 and 27-inch monitors 2560 x 1440.

So for example, if you need, or are comfortable with, a resolution of 1280 x 1024, your choice will be restricted to 17- and 19-inch models.

Pixel Response Rate

This specification indicates how quickly a pixel can change color and it is measured in milliseconds (ms). The lower the figure, the faster the response rate. A sufficiently fast response rate is critical for eliminating or reducing the blurring effect you might otherwise see in a moving or changing image on an LCD monitor.

In order to eliminate completely any ghosting/blurring, a monitor's pixel response rate must be no higher than 16 ms.

Viewing Angles

CRT monitors could be viewed from any angle and while the sharper the angle the less you saw, the image itself didn't deteriorate. This is not the case with LCDs. With these there is a noticeable loss of image quality when the monitor is viewed at an angle. Note that the viewing-angle problem is more pronounced as LCD size increases.

Connections

All modern monitors provide a digital DVI port for connection to the PC. Many also provide the older analogue VGA port but these are becoming less common. So if your PC's video system doesn't provide a DVI connection, make sure your new monitor comes with a VGA port.

Alternatively, you can also buy a video card that provides DVI. This needn't be an expensive model – low-end cards can be picked up for around $20 or so.

Hot tip

More recent monitors may have a High-Definition Multimedia Interface (HDMI) connector. The purpose of this is to provide a connection for consumer video equipment such as Blu-ray players, TVs, etc. If you don't intend to use your PC for this type of purpose though, a DVI connection is all you'll need.

Another type of interface now being seen on high-end monitors is the DisplayPort interface. This has been developed to eventually replace the DVI interface.

Connecting an LCD Monitor

LCD monitors can be connected to the system via either VGA, DVI or DisplayPort connections. Currently, most PC systems and monitors use DVI so this is what we are using below to illustrate the procedure.

Hot tip

If your PC only provides a VGA video output, you can buy a VGA to DVI adaptor that enables you to connect it to a DVI equipped monitor.

Monitor connected to a video card DVI port

Beware

If your PC has both a video card and integrated video, make sure that you connect the monitor to the correct system. This is a very common mistake and is easily done.

Monitor connected to a video card VGA port

Printers

To meet their printing requirements, upgraders have a choice of four types of device. These are:

- Inkjet printers
- Laser printers
- Photo printers
- Multi-function devices (MFDs)

Beware

Manufacturers rate the print speed of their printers in pages per minute (PPM). However, these are taken under optimal printing conditions and do not reflect their real-world performance. Take these with a pinch of salt – the real print speed will be considerably less.

Inkjet Printers

Cheap and readily available, these devices are the ideal solution for all-round, or occasional, printing requirements. Print quality, while not the best, is perfectly adequate for most purposes.

They do, however, have some limitations that make them unsuitable for high-quality or large scale printing.

Don't forget

If you do serious amounts of printing, an inkjet will be a slow and expensive way of doing it.

- Inkjets are not the quickest printers; in fact many of them are painfully slow at anything other than draft quality. For the odd letter now and then they are fine but for more serious printing, their slow print speed can be very restrictive

- Inkjets may be available at low prices but this definitely does not apply to the consumables (ink cartridges, paper, etc). These are highly priced and this is where the manufacturers make their money

Beware

The head cleaning utilities provided with inkjets work by forcing ink through the print nozzles to clear any blockages. This is another common cause of contamination (they also use a lot of extremely expensive ink in the process).

- Inkjets can be messy devices and this is due to the fact that they work by literally firing the ink at the paper. It is quite common with these devices for ink to contaminate the platen and rollers, which is then transferred to the paper in the form of smudges and streaks

Should you decide to buy one of these printers, consider the following:

Print Resolution – this is expressed in dots per inch (dpi). Letter quality begins at 300 dpi but a higher figure will be required for the highest quality printing. Photographs print acceptably at 300 dpi. All inkjets provide 300 dpi but the resolution offered will be worth checking if you need really high quality printing.

Print Speed – this is rated in pages per minute (PPM) and as we mentioned on the previous page, it does not give an accurate indication. However, it can be useful as a rough guide when comparing different models.

Paper Handling – mainstream inkjets will print letter size or lower. If you need to print larger documents, you will need to buy a business class inkjet, which will be considerably more expensive. Another thing to look at if you envisage having long print jobs is the capacity of the paper input tray. Low-end inkjets will hold no more than 50 sheets or so; high-end models will hold about 150.

Photo Printers

Due to the popularity of PCs for storing and editing images, photo printers are now extremely popular. These use inkjet

Hot tip

Note that some photo printers are not so good at printing text, as they are designed for smooth color blending rather than sharp lines. That said, if your requirements aren't too high in this respect, most of them are adequate.

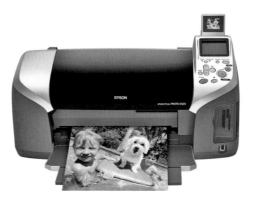

technology but take it to a different level in terms of print quality. One of the ways they achieve this is by using a wider range of colored inks than standard inkjets do. As a result, print quality approaches that of professional print labs.

Photo printers are also much quicker than standard inkjets, which can take an eternity to print a high-quality photo. Another feature they offer is the ability to read directly from flash memory cards, such as those used by digital cameras. This means that the PC is bypassed completely. Many also offer an LCD to view your photos, not to mention editing facilities such as crop, rotate, brightness and contrast adjustment, etc.

Things to look out for when buying a photo printer include:

Ink Cartridges – photo printers use between four and six different inks and generally, the ones that use six will produce higher quality prints than those which use less.

Be aware that cheaper models may use a single cartridge that contains all the inks, so if one color runs out, the cartridge has to be replaced even though the other colors haven't. Therefore, running costs can be cut substantially by choosing a model in which each color is held in a separate cartridge.

Memory Card Reader – if you want to take advantage of the direct printing facility offered by these printers, make sure it can read the type of memory card that you use.

Print Size – many photo printers have a maximum print size of 4 x 6 inches, which is fine for snapshots. If you want larger sizes, say to frame and hang on the wall, you may need a more expensive model.

Laser Printers

Lasers use a completely different technology than inkjets, which produces a higher level of print quality and speed. They also offer much more in the way of features, such as duplexing (the ability to print on both sides of the page) and high-capacity paper input trays. Furthermore, they have much lower running costs.

Traditionally, these devices have been superb at printing text but not so good at color images, as print resolutions were often limited to 600 dpi (which is fine for text).

However, with more and more users demanding photo quality from their laser printers, the manufacturers are now providing models that print at 1200 dpi.

Beware

Not all printers with the word "photo" in their name are actually photo printers. Some are merely a general-purpose printer with a few photo printer features, such as direct printing from memory cards or the ability to make borderless prints. Study the specs carefully to weed out the jokers.

153

...cont'd

While these do produce good-quality color prints, it must be said that low-end color lasers still cannot match an inkjet photo printer.

The price of laser printers has dropped considerably over the last few years and it is now possible to buy a black & white model for less than $100, which is less than a high-end inkjet will cost.

However, buyers should be aware that if they buy one of these low-cost models, they will be buying at the bottom of the laser market and the performance offered may be no better than that of a good quality inkjet. Probably the only benefit will be lower running costs.

When buying a laser printer, consider the following:

Print Resolution – for text, a dpi of 600 is fine. However, if you intend to print color photos, a dpi of 1200 is recommended. Note that low-end color lasers offer a dpi of only 600.

Consumables – while these are much cheaper than inkjet consumables, you can make further savings by buying a model that has the toner (laser equivalent to inkjet ink) in a separate cartridge. Some lasers have the toner and the drum (which needs to be replaced much less frequently) combined in a single cartridge. As the toner runs out long before it is necessary to replace the drum, being able to replace each individually is more cost-effective.

Memory – lasers come equipped with memory. However, low-end models aren't equipped with much, often only enough for small-scale print jobs and low-resolution photo printing. Make sure that the model you buy allows you to install extra memory (not all do), should it be necessary.

Beware

Keep your eyes peeled for laser printers that claim an "effective" resolution of 1200 dpi. This means a real resolution of 600 dpi that has been bumped-up by means of software enhancement. This is a way (much favored by manufacturers of printers (and scanners)), to make their products appear better than they actually are.

Multi-Function Devices (MFDs)

These devices consist of a printer and a scanner, which also combine to act as a copier, and sometimes a fax machine, all incorporated within the same housing.

The advantages offered are convenience (one connection to the PC, one wall socket required), less desktop space than would be required by stand-alone devices, and a cost-saving compared to buying the devices separately.

Along with the lower price, however, you will usually also get lower quality, unless you opt for a high-end model, in which case you will lose the cost-saving. The advice then is to steer clear of MFDs unless: a) space is at a premium, and b) you can afford a high-end model that will meet your requirements.

To this end, you should study the specifications for each incorporated device as you would with stand-alone devices.

The bottom line then:

- For high-quality glossy photographs, an inkjet photo printer will be the best choice. If high-quality text printing is also a requirement, it may be necessary to buy a low-end laser printer as well

- For large-scale text based print jobs, a laser is the recommended option. Even a low-end model will be better than inkjets, with the added advantage of much lower running costs

- For the busy home office where print jobs are frequent, and use both text and color, a low-end color laser will be a real boon. Not only will printing be quicker and cheaper; more options will be available, such as being able to print on both sides of a page. In short, productivity will be much increased

- If space and/or cost is an issue, and high quality isn't, go for a multi-function device

Beware

A potential problem with multi-function devices is that if they go wrong, the user may lose all the functions that they provide.

Installing a Printer

The usual procedure with modern printers is to install the driver first. Then you connect the device to the computer (demonstrated below) and switch it on when instructed to do so by the installation procedure. The printer is then configured automatically.

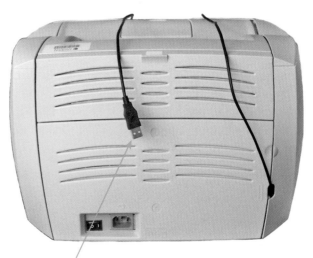

1 Take the USB cable from the printer and connect it to a USB port on the PC

11 Better Network Connections

In this chapter, we investigate Internet connection options. We also take a look at the subject of home networking.

Broadband

Those of you still laboriously accessing the Internet via a dial-up connection (25 per cent of American households still use dial-up), might care to consider upgrading your Internet connection to broadband.

The following options are available:

Cable

This utilizes CATV cable networks (cable TV) and currently offers speeds up to a maximum of 100 Mbps, depending on where in the world you live. It is also the most reliable type of broadband connection as most cables are underground where they are not subject to storm and other types of damage.

ADSL

ADSL works by separating the bandwidth of telephone lines into several frequency ranges, known as carriers. As each carrier can transmit a different type of signal independently of the other carriers, it is possible for one telephone line to support surfing the web, watching streaming video, telephone calls, etc, simultaneously.

ADSL connections offer similar speeds to cable but are not as reliable.

ISDN

ISDN is very similar to dial-up connections in that users have to dial a number to establish a connection. However, it is twice as fast as dial-up, offering a maximum speed of 128 Kbps. Its other advantage over dial-up is that it allows Internet access and telephone calls simultaneously. Other than that there is little to be said for it.

Satellite

This is an option for those who can't get a fast Internet connection via the methods mentioned above. Satellite broadband is available at speeds up to about 8 Mbps.

However, there are issues: First, it is the most expensive type of broadband and second, because the signal has to travel to the satellite and back to earth again, a latency (delay) of about 1,000–1,400 ms will be experienced by the user.

Hot tip

If you are fortunate enough to have a choice, cable broadband is the recommended option. It's quick, reliable, and easy to set up.

Installing a Broadband Modem

The first step is to extend the signal input from its entry point at the house to where the modem is located. For this you will need a suitable length of coaxial cable and the appropriate connectors. If you are tapping into your TV's cable input, you will also need a signal splitter, as shown left. Connect the signal cable to the splitter's input, connect the TV to one output and the modem's cable to the other output. Then run the latter to the modem.

Hot tip

If you are using an Ethernet modem, you will also need an Ethernet adaptor in the PC. There may be one built-in to the motherboard, in which case you will have to install the Ethernet driver from the motherboard's installation disk. Otherwise, you will need to buy and install a separate adaptor.

1 Connect the power cable

2 Connect the interface cable

3 Connect the signal input

4 Connect the modem (a USB modem in this example) to the PC.

Beware

When running your new modem for the first time, remember that it may need several minutes to synchronize itself with the network. During this period, you will be unable to access the Internet.

5 Switch the PC on and when back in Windows run the installation disk. In the case of a USB modem, the USB driver required by the modem will be installed automatically. The software will then establish and configure your broadband connection

Home Networking

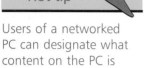

Users looking to modernise their existing setup might consider upgrading it to a home network. A network is basically a number of computers (or devices such as printers, cameras, etc) that are connected by either a cable (known as a wired network) or a radio link (known as a wireless network). Any type, or combination, of computer and associated devices can be used in this way.

The users of networked PCs/devices have direct access to all the other PCs and devices on the network, thus allowing the contents and resources of each to be shared. If user A needs a file that is on user B's PC, it can be simply copied across. If only one of the PCs in the network has a printer connected to it, all the other PCs can use this printer.

In a home environment, these features, and others, can be extremely useful in many ways. One such is the facility to share a single internet connection with a number of PCs located in different rooms.

A good example of this in use is the kids using the Internet to do their homework. Son and daughter can both engage in this activity without having to wait for the other to finish. At the same time, Dad can be checking his emails or catching up on the baseball results. The inevitable conflicts that arise from having to share the connection are eliminated.

A network can also be used as the basis of a home entertainment center enabling video and audio to be piped around the house from one location.

If the network is wireless, it is much more flexible. For example, if it's a nice day you can take your laptop out into the garden and browse the Internet from there. Networked devices can be moved to different locations without having to reroute cabling.

Wireless hotspots (see margin note) enable the user to access the network from literally anywhere in the world. If you go out forgetting to record your favorite TV program, you can do it from whereever you are via your home network and a hotspot.

The advantages and uses provided by a home network are clear. In the following pages, we'll take a brief look at the various types of network.

Building a Home Network

Cable Networks

The traditional method is by using specialized network cable that connects to a network adaptor in each of the networked devices. With large networks, such as are found in corporate environments, this is no easy task as it requires a thorough knowledge of network topology (types of configuration and associated pros and cons), and devices such as routers and access points.

In a home environment though, it is a relatively straightforward task as each device is simply linked to the next one. The main problem involves the routing of the cable. If you are handy with an electric drill, and are comfortable with the prospect of pulling up floorboards and recessing the cable into the walls, go ahead. No matter how handy you are though, a certain amount of remodelling will be necessary.

The advantages of this type of network are speed and reliability. Network cable offers the fastest possible data transfer speeds, and once in place the system will be extremely reliable as the cable is durable, and also shielded against electrical interference. The only thing that's likely to go wrong is a dodgy connection to one of the devices, which is easily and quickly remedied.

Power Cable Networks

A much easier, and less messy, type of system known as HomePlug, uses the house's power cables. This is available in kits consisting of two or more HomePlug adaptors, an installation disc and all the necessary connection cables. All you have to do is plug each adaptor into the nearest wall socket, connect them to network adaptors in the PCs and run the installation disc. As every room has at least one wall socket, there should be no need to install any wiring at all, apart from maybe an extension cable from the socket to the PC.

Beware

Network cable is approximately a quarter of an inch in diameter, so don't think that you will be able to get away with running it under the carpets.

Don't forget

The disadvantage of HomePlug networks is that their data transfer capabilities are much less than other types of network.

If all you want is to share an Internet connection, and simple file sharing, they are adequate. However, they may not provide enough bandwidth for sharing audio and video files.

...cont'd

Telephone Wire Networks

A system very similar to HomePlug, called HomePNA, makes use of the telephone wiring in the house. Again, this is supplied in kits comprising a number of adaptors, connection cables and software.

The ease of setting it up depends on whether you have telephone jacks near enough to the PCs to be networked. If you don't though, these are simple enough to install with the aid of extension kits. Plus, the cables can be run under carpets.

Wireless Networks

Also known as Wi-Fi, this is the easiest way to set up a home network, assuming that you are running a recent version of Windows. A wireless network can be set up with other operating

systems but it is a more difficult and protracted procedure. The network wizard provided by Windows does the job with a few clicks of the mouse.

All that's required in the way of hardware is a wireless network adaptor for each PC/device to be networked. This can be either an internally installed card or an external USB device.

Apart from the ease of setting them up, the great advantages of wireless networks are their flexibility, and the range of uses to which they can be put. With regard to the latter, there are now any number of wireless devices on the market, such as LCD TVs, music systems, and cameras.

By incorporating them into a wireless network, these devices can be simply picked up and moved to wherever they are needed.

12 Fixing Your PC

The faults highlighted in this chapter are mainly restricted to the ones most likely to be experienced as a result of a component upgrade. As Windows 7 is currently the most popular operating system, the screenshots and troubleshooting procedures (where applicable), are taken from this version of Windows.

Initial Steps

This chapter is intended mainly as a troubleshooting aid for when an upgrade has gone wrong. However, it also covers more general types of computer fault that may occur at any time.

In practice, it is virtually impossible to repair a computer hardware device without specialized electronic equipment, e.g. an oscilloscope (plus the knowledge of how to use it). Because of this, computer hardware devices are repaired by the simple expedient of replacement with a working model. This is what repair technicians do and it is simple enough – the difficult part is pin-pointing the faulty device.

One reason for this is the fact that many PC faults can have several causes and this makes it difficult to know where to start. A very useful pointer here is that the majority of faults are actually induced by the user, often as a result of doing something incorrectly, or that shouldn't have been done at all.

So the first thing to do is cast your mind back to what you were doing on the PC prior to the fault materializing. Very often this will provide you with a starting point. The following activities are the cause of most problems.

Installing and Uninstalling Software
Software installation can introduce bugs, malware/viruses, and incompatibility issues with other software, particularly the operating system. Uninstalling software can also uninstall files needed by other programs.

Using the Internet and Email
Both of these activities can introduce malware and viruses.

Installing Hardware
Hardware drivers can be the cause of configuration problems with other hardware devices. If the hardware is an internal device, it can also be the cause of heat issues. Another potential cause of problems is dislodging the connections of other devices during the installation.

Changing BIOS and System Settings
This can cause a whole range of faults.

Incorrect Shutting Down of the PC
This can corrupt the PC's file system, and Windows startup files.

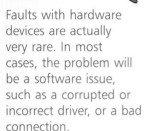

Troubleshooting Tools

Before you do any upgrading, you should familiarize yourself with the diagnostic and repair tools provided by Windows in case of subsequent problems.

Device Manager

Technically, this is not a troubleshooting tool. However, it does indicate when a hardware device has a problem and so can be useful. Access and use the utility as follows:

1 Windows Vista users should go to Start, Control Panel, System and Maintenance, System, Device Manager. Windows 7 users will find the Device Manager in the Control Panel

2 Here you see a list of every hardware device installed on the PC

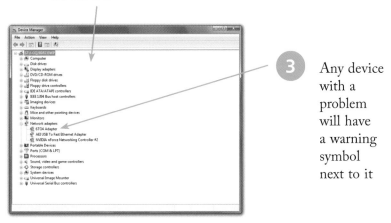

3 Any device with a problem will have a warning symbol next to it

4 Double-click the device to see the nature of the problem and the suggested remedy

...cont'd

Windows Advanced Options

The Windows Advanced Options Menu provides three very useful troubleshooting tools and can be accessed by booting the PC and then tapping the F8 key. After a few moments, the Windows Advanced Options Menu will open as shown below:

```
Windows Advanced Options Menu
Please select An Option

Safe Mode
Safe Mode With Networking
Safe Mode With Command Prompt

Enable Boot Logging
Enable VGA Mode
Last Known Good Configuration (Your Most Recent Settings That Worked)
Directory Services Restore Mode (Windows Domain Controllers Only)

Start Windows Normally
Reboot
Return To OS Choices Menu

Use the up and down arrow keys to move the highlight to your choice
```

Don't forget

If you are unable to get Windows started, reboot the PC into Safe Mode; this should get it going. However, be aware that when in Safe Mode, Windows will run much more slowly than usual and many of its functions will be disabled. Its troubleshooting tools will be accessible, though.

Safe Mode – this is used to troubleshoot hardware problems that prevent Windows from starting. It works by bypassing the normal Windows configuration, instead loading a "stripped-down" version with a set of basic drivers. Anything that is not essential in getting the system operational is not loaded, e.g. audio devices, peripherals, and devices connected via USB ports. Also, all startup programs are ignored while Safe Mode is activated.

As a result, most of the issues likely to stop Windows from starting are eliminated.

When the PC is running in Safe Mode, the user can access most essential repair and configuration tools, including Device Manager, System Restore, Registry Editor, and Backup. Virtually all Help and Support Center features are available in Safe Mode as well.

This enables the user to investigate the issue and hopefully resolve it. For example, if you suspect that a newly installed device driver may be the cause of the problem, you will be able to "roll back" to the previous driver in the Device Manager. In the case of a newly installed application, you can use the "Programs and Features" applet in the Control Panel to uninstall it.

Last Known Good Configuration – when selected, this option will boot the PC with the registry information and driver settings that were in effect the last time the computer was started successfully. If your computer starts, i.e. you can see text on the boot screen (which indicates your hardware is OK) but fails to boot into Windows, this option is the first thing to try.

Enable VGA Mode – this starts Windows with a very low desktop resolution of 640 x 480, and a refresh rate of 60 hz, by using the current video driver. This mode is useful for resolving video related issues.

A typical example of this is when the user has been messing around with resolutions and/or refresh rates and has selected one that the monitor can't display. This often results in a garbled or blank display, which prevents the user from reverting back to a setting that works. Booting into VGA Mode will restore a picture and allow the user to choose a setting that works.

If you need access to network connections, choose the Safe Mode with Networking option, which loads the basic set of Safe Mode files and adds drivers and services required to start Windows networking, i.e. the Internet.

Chkdsk

Chkdsk is a utility that checks the hard drive for physical errors, such as bad sectors and, more importantly, the PC's file system. It will also repair any problems that it finds. Good indicators of a corrupted file system are general system instability, file copy errors and loss of data. Whenever you experience any of these problems, you should run Chkdsk.

To do it, open My Computer and right-click the drive you want to check. Select Properties and then click the Tools tab. Under Error checking, click Check Now and then in the new window check "Automatically fix file system errors". Then click Start.

Note that if the drive being checked is the one on which Windows is installed, you will need to restart the PC for the check to take place.

Hot tip

Chkdsk should also be run after an incorrect shutdown. This is the most common cause of file system errors.

System Restore

Versions of Windows from Me onwards, provide a utility called System Restore. This utility takes "snapshots" (called restore points) of the entire system whenever major changes are made to it, such as a program being installed or uninstalled. These snapshots are saved and can be used to restore the system to the state it was in when the snapshot was taken.

This is an extremely useful way of repairing a software fault without having to go to the bother of locating it, and will resolve many issues. System Restore, however, is of no use with regard to hardware faults and if you have reason to suspect your hardware, there is no point in running it.

1 Go to Start, All Programs, Accessories, System Tools and System Restore

2 At the first screen, click "Restore my computer to an earlier time"

3 Select an appropriate restore point and click Next. Windows will restore the system and then reboot to complete the procedure

The Power Supply

As we have mentioned previously, power supply units are one of the hardware devices most likely to cause trouble. Usually, they leave the user in no doubt – a loud bang accompanied by a wisp of smoke, which is pretty conclusive. However, nothing in life is certain, so if your PC appears to be dead, you have to check the power supply first, bang or no bang.

Before you do, establish that the PC really is dead. There are three things to check:

1) The LEDs at the front of the case are all off

2) The keyboards LEDs are off

3) The power supply unit, CPU and case fans are not running

If none of the above are working then the PC is not receiving any power. Troubleshoot by checking the following:

- Confirm that there is power at the wall socket by plugging an appliance such as a hairdryer into it. If the appliance works, the socket is OK

- Bypass any device that is connected between the wall socket and the PSU, such as a surge suppressor or cable extension

- Check the PC's power cable by replacing it with one known to be good (you may have a household appliance that uses the same type)

- Check that the on/off switch at the rear of the PSU hasn't been switched to the off position inadvertently. This is not unlikely if children have been in the vicinity recently

If the computer is still not powering up after carrying out these checks, the power supply unit has failed and will have to be replaced.

A less easy type of PSU fault to diagnose is when the device is producing current outputs that fluctuate – this can be the cause of inexplicable lock-ups and crashes. If you find yourself experiencing an unusual amount of these, the PSU is the first thing to suspect. For most people, the only way of establishing this for certain is to replace the device with a new model.

Don't forget

Don't overlook the on/off switch on the PSU. What's out of sight is often out of mind. Many users are not even aware that it exists.

System Hardware

By system hardware, we mean essential hardware devices without which the PC will not start. These are:

- The motherboard
- The video system
- Memory

If any of these are faulty, bootup will either not start at all or stop at the boot screen.

Motherboard

This system component is the most difficult one of all to troubleshoot as it may be one of the components connected to the board that is actually the cause of the problem, e.g. CPU, memory.

One of the problems most likely to face a user who has just upgraded their motherboard is switching on only to be greeted by a blank screen. In this situation, check the following:

Is the PC making an unusual beeping noise. If it is, you are hearing a beep code – all the major parts of a PC have beep codes that indicate a problem – see page 173 for more on this subject.

Is the monitor connected to the PC and if so is it connected to the correct video socket? Is it even switched on?

Is the board receiving power? – indications that it is are: operational CPU fan, lit LEDs on the motherboard, case front panel and the keyboard. If it is not powered up, check you have connected the 24-pin power supply from the PSU. If this appears to be ok, you have almost certainly damaged the board by careless handling and it will have to be replaced.

If the board is powered up, the next thing to check is the CPU's power supply. This is a separate 12 volt supply from the PSU, without which it, and hence the PC, won't work. Make sure this is connected – it's a 4- or 8-pin (8-pin on modern high-end CPUs) connector.

If this checks out as well, make sure the PC's on/off switch is connected correctly.

If everything with the motherboard seems to be as it should, the system's memory is the next thing to check.

Hot tip

As far as the upgrader is concerned, problems with any of these devices will usually be restricted to connection issues. The beep codes will tell you which device has a problem; just check the relevant connections.

Hot tip

The socket for the CPU's 12 volt supply will be located close to the CPU.

Memory

Memory faults can result in a blank screen. They can also be the cause of bootup stopping on the first boot screen at the memory test stage. When either happens, you should hear a memory specific beep code or simply a continuous beeping.

In either case, the first thing to check is that the memory module is installed in the correct slot. In most motherboards, when a single memory module is being used it must be installed in a particular slot, not just any one. In the case of two or more modules installed in a dual- or triple-channel configuration, they must be installed in a certain order. This information will be in the motherboard manual.

While on the subject of multi-channel memory, many motherboards designed for this type of memory configuration will not work unless all the channels have a module installed in them, i.e. a triple-channel motherboard must have three modules. Furthermore, many of these motherboards provide two dual- or triple-channel circuits. The former will thus provide four memory slots – two for each circuit while the latter will provide six slots – three for each circuit. In this situation, the slots for each circuit will be a different color and if you are only going to use one of the circuits, the modules must be installed in the correct slots for that circuit.

Be aware that memory modules are easily damaged by the electrostatic electricity in your body and must be handled with care. Think back to when you installed the module. Did you handle it correctly by grounding yourself first and then holding it at the edges, or did you touch the circuits on the module without first grounding yourself? If it's the latter, you can assume the module is damaged and will thus need replacing.

Another memory related problem that upgraders can come across is buying modules that just don't work with the motherboard. Technically, they may be compatible but in practise the motherboard simply refuses to work with them, or vice versa. This issue can be avoided by making sure the memory you buy is recommended for use with the motherboard in your system. This information will be available at the manufacturers' websites.

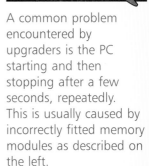

Hot tip

A common problem encountered by upgraders is the PC starting and then stopping after a few seconds, repeatedly. This is usually caused by incorrectly fitted memory modules as described on the left.

The Video System

If the motherboard, CPU, memory and monitor are all operational, a blank screen can have only one cause – lack of video.

As we have seen in chapter 7, a PC's video is provided by either a dedicated video card or a video system integrated in the motherboard. Whichever you are using, a fault should be signalled by a beep code.

If you are using a video card, the first thing to check is that it is securely connected to the motherboard. In the case of a PCI-Express video card, which will require a dedicated power supply from the PSU, make sure that this is present and correct. An operational video card cooling fan will be your confirmation of this.

Next check that the monitor is connected to it. If your system has both integrated video and a video card, make sure the monitor is connected to the video card and not the integrated video.

Hot tip

If you can see anything on the screen – even a single dot – the video system is operational.

Hot tip

If your PC has both an integrated video system and a video card, you can use one to check the other.

Video card

Integrated video

Note that having both a video card and integrated video provides a foolproof means of fault isolation. All you have to do is switch the monitor connection to the integrated video system. If you now have video, you know the issue lies with the video card and, if everything else checks out, the card must be faulty.

Beep Codes

Beep codes are a series of beeps, which are so named because they have a meaning. Each code is different and indicates a fault (usually non-specific) with major components of a PC. These codes provide a useful way of identifying faulty devices.

Before you can decipher the beep codes, you will need to know the manufacturer of the BIOS chip in your system. The reason for this is that it is the BIOS that produces the beep codes and different BIOS manufacturers use different codes. You will find this information in the PC's documentation. It should also be specified at the top of the first screen.

The following tables show an abbreviated list of the most common beep codes (see margin note).

AMI BIOS	
Beeps	**Faulty Device**
1, 2 or 3	Memory (RAM). Reseat the module. If that doesn't work, replace it
4 to 7, 9 to 11	Motherboard or expansion card. Remove all the expansion cards; if the system still beeps, the motherboard is faulty. Otherwise, one of the expansion cards is faulty
8	Video System

AWARD BIOS	
Beeps	**Faulty Device**
1	This is normal and indicates that everything is OK
1 long, 2 short	Video system
Any other sequence	Memory

NOTE: if you have an AWARD BIOS in your system, you will hear a single beep when switching on. This indicates everything is normal. If you don't hear it, you almost certainly have a faulty motherboard.

However, this does not apply to AMI BIOSs – a single beep when switching on indicates a memory fault.

Hard Drives

When you start the computer, on the first boot screen you should see the hard drive listed (the Samsung HD103SJ in the example below). If it is, this indicates that the BIOS has recognized the drive and configured it correctly.

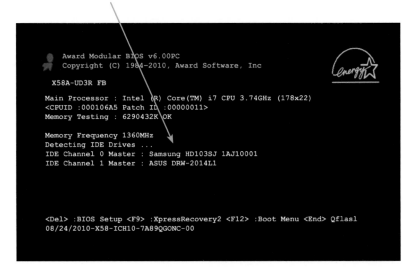

If it isn't there, the BIOS isn't "seeing" it. Depending on the BIOS in your system, one of two things will happen.

1) Boot-up will stop at this point

2) Boot-up will continue and then stop with a "Disk Boot Failure" error message

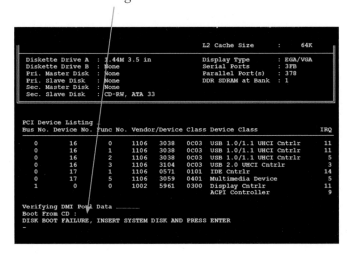

With regard to the former, there are three possible causes:

1) The drive is not connected correctly
2) The drive is not powered up
3) The drive is faulty

The first thing to check is that the drive is connected to the motherboard. Remake the interface connections and check that they are correct.

Then check the drive is getting power from the power supply unit. The easiest way to do this is to connect a different power connector that you know is working; for example, the one powering the CD/DVD drive.

If the drive is getting power and the connections are OK, then the device is faulty. This is very unlikely though and invariably the fault will be a connection issue.

In the case of a Disk Boot Failure error message, the usual cause is that the system is configured to boot from a non-boot drive. This is particularly likely if you have two or more hard drives in the system. Check it out as follows:

Go into the BIOS, open the Advanced Features page, select "Hard Disk Boot Priority" and make sure the boot drive (the one Windows is installed on) is specified as the first drive.

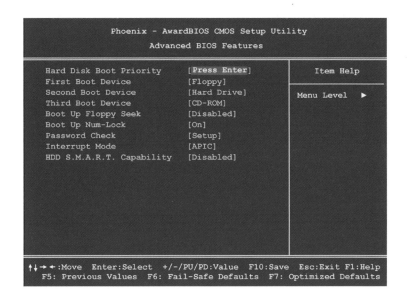

Don't forget

If you install two or more hard drives in your system, remember to check that the boot drive has priority in the BIOS. This is the drive on which the BIOS will expect to find the operating system.

...cont'd

Another problem that can occur is the boot procedure stopping at the "Verifying DMI Pool Data" stage. DMI pool data is hardware related information that is passed from the BIOS to the operating system during bootup, and if the BIOS finds an error during the verification stage, the boot procedure may stop at this point.

```
                                          L2 Cache Size       :      64K

Diskette Drive A  : 1.44M 3.5 in          Display Type        : EGA/VGA
Diskette Drive B  : None                  Serial Ports        : 3FB
Pri. Master Disk  : None                  Parallel Port(s)    : 378
Pri. Slave Disk   : None                  DDR SDRAM at Bank   : 1
Sec. Master Disk  : None
Sec. Slave Disk   : CD-RW, ATA 33


PCI Device Listing …
Bus No. Device No. Func No.  Vendor/Device Class Device Class                IRQ
     0       16        0      1106   3038   0C03  USB 1.0/1.1 UHCI Cntrlr    11
     0       16        1      1106   3038   0C03  USB 1.0/1.1 UHCI Cntrlr    11
     0       16        2      1106   3038   0C03  USB 1.0/1.1 UHCI Cntrlr     5
     0       16        3      1106   3104   0C03  USB 2.0 UHCI Cntrlr         3
     0       17        1      1106   0571   0101  IDE Cntrlr                 14
     0       17        5      1106   3059   0401  Multimedia Device           5
     1        0        0      1002   5961   0300  Display Cntrlr             11
                                              ACPI Controller                9

Verifying DMI Pool Data …………….
     -
```

The usual cause is a connection issue but it can also be the result of a transient configuration problem that can be resolved by simply switching off and then back on again. This is the first thing to try. If the problem persists, however, you almost certainly have a bad connection somewhere.

Check the drive's connections and try again. If the boot procedure still hangs, disconnect all non-boot drives, i.e. DVD drives, external hard drives, flash drives, as it's possible the system is trying to boot from one of them rather than the boot drive.

If there is still no joy, reseat all expansion boards connected to the PC, e.g. sound and video cards, TV tuner cards, etc.

The last resort is to replace the drive.

Video

On page 172, we looked at video related issues that can be the cause of a blank display when the PC is booted. These are the types of problem that users upgrading a video card will, typically, face. On this page, we will check out some other, more general, types of video problems.

One of the most common is also the result of a video card upgrade. In this scenario, the PC boots up ok but then stops with a blank screen at the point where Windows begins to load. This is often caused by the system trying to assign the video driver used by the original video system to the new video card. The result is known as a hardware conflict and can be prevented by uninstalling the old video driver before installing the new card. However, if you've already made this mistake, the solution is to use Safe Mode as described on page 166 to get back into Windows and then uninstall the old driver.

Another mistake sometimes made by upgraders is to forget (or even be unaware of the necessity), to install the video card driver at all. This results in the video being so slow that you can literally see it being drawn on the screen. You will also find that the display's resolution and color depth cannot be changed.

A problem that can occur with LCD monitors is a poor quality display where images become blocky and text loses its sharpness. This is caused by the user changing the monitor's resolution from the native resolution to one that's lower. Without going too much into this, LCD monitors can only produce a high quality picture at their native, or fixed, resolution. The solution is to simply reselect the monitor's native resolution.

If a user selects a resolution that is too high, i.e. that the monitor cannot display at all, the result will be a completely garbled display. The solution to this is to reboot the PC in Safe Mode, which will restore a basic picture, and thus allow the user to select a lower resolution that the monitor can display.

Finally, it is a fact that very few users have their monitor set up correctly in terms of color balance, gamma, brilliance and contrast. While this is not a video issue as such, it is related in that the video system's output is inaccurately displayed by the monitor. This is very easy to remedy by using the monitor calibration utility provided by Windows 7 – see margin note.

Hot tip

Access the Windows 7 monitor calibration utility by going to the Control Panel and clicking Display. On the left, click "Calibrate Color".

Sound

A new sound card has been installed but unfortunately it's not producing any.

The first thing to check is that the PC's integrated sound system has been disabled. See page 65 for instructions on how to do this.

Then check that the system has recognized the card. Do this by opening the Device Manager and expanding the "Sound, video and game controllers" category. You should see your sound card listed here (Creative SB X-Fi in the example below):

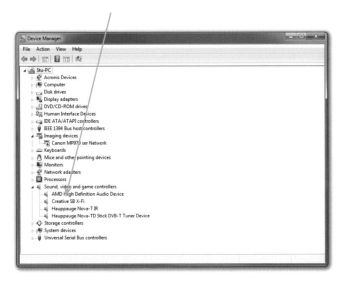

If it's not, make sure it is securely connected to the motherboard. Did you install the card's driver? If not, doing so will resolve the problem. Once, or if, the card is listed in the Device Manager, but you still have no sound, check the following:

Are the speakers connected to the integrated sound system rather than to the sound card? – this is an easy mistake to make.

Are the speakers connected to the correct output jack – this will be stamped as Line Out, Speaker Out or Audio Out.

If you are using powered speakers, are they powered up?

Finally, check that the volume controls, both on the speakers and in Windows, are turned up.

In a situation where the sound has been working and then suddenly stopped, suspect the sound system's driver immediately.

1 Go to Start, Control Panel, Sound. Then click the Audio tab

Sound system drivers are notorious for corruption. If your PC suddenly loses its sound, this is the first thing to check.

179

2 If there is nothing listed under the Playback and Recording tabs then the driver is either corrupted or hasn't been installed

3 Reinstall the driver to restore the sound

Don't forget

System Restore is an ideal way of quickly resolving a sound system driver issue.

If the driver is OK, the problem is hardware related. Check the speakers and their connections as per the previous page.

If the sound is still not working, in the case of an integrated system, the motherboard will need to be replaced. A more practical solution, however, would be to simply buy a sound card.

In the case of a sound card, connect the speakers to the PC's integrated system (after enabling it in the BIOS). If it works now, there is a problem with the sound card. Check that it is securely connected to the motherboard; failing that it will have to be replaced.

Broadband

You've just installed a modem, hooked it up to your broadband connection, switched on, fired-up your browser and .... nothing. All you see is "This page cannot be displayed".

Check the following:

LEDs – all broadband modems have a number of LEDs, each of which indicate something specific. Unfortunately, no two modems are the same in this respect so we can't help you on this – you'll need to consult the documentation.

Hot tip

Occasionally, broadband modems will lose contact with the ISP. This can be due to a problem at the ISP's end or to a power outage at the user's end; there are other causes as well.

Whichever, the user loses his connection. The solution to this problem is to "power cycle" the modem. Do it as follows:

Switch the PC off, disconnect the modem and then reconnect it before switching the PC back on. Without going into the reasons, this will very often re-establish your connection.

Look for the LED that indicates whether or not the modem is receiving data. If it is lit, this tells you that the ISP's servers are OK, and that the incoming connection to the modem is as well. If it is not, either your ISP's servers are down (contact them to verify this) or there is a bad connection between the cable input to the house and the modem.

Then check the LED that indicates a good connection between the modem and the PC. If this is out, make sure the cable is plugged in securely at both ends. If you are using a USB modem, check that USB is enabled in the BIOS (see page 63).

Modem driver – open Device Manager and make sure that the modem is listed under Network Adapters. If not, reinstall its driver. If there is a warning symbol next to the modem, double-click it to see what the problem is.

Software – reinstall the ISP's software from the installation disk. If there is still no joy, you should find a diagnostic utility on the installation disk; most ISPs supply one. These utilities can resolve software configuration issues.

As a last resort, you'll have to contact the ISP's technical support.

Monitors

Faults with these devices are very rare but when they do occur, will be either a total failure or some sort of image distortion. Fortunately, particularly in the case of expensive monitors, they can be repaired and there are many repair shops available for this purpose.

With regard to image problems, you don't need a degree to figure this one out. Troubleshooting a blank display isn't too difficult either. The first thing to check (as with all electrical or electronic equipment) is the power supply; if the front panel LED is lit, the device has power, if it isn't, it doesn't have power. In the latter case, check that there is power at the wall socket and that the power cord (including the fuse in the plug) is sound, and firmly connected.

If the LED is lit, the monitor is either in standby mode, in which case pressing the on/off button once will bring it to life, or it is in power management mode. Pressing a key or clicking the mouse should return it to normal operation.

Note that in some systems, the power management mode may be reluctant to relinquish its grip and a considerable amount of key bashing or mouse clicking may be necessary.

If the screen is still blank, switch off both the PC and the monitor, and then disconnect the VGA or DVI cable from the video system.

Switch the monitor back on and if you now see a test signal, as shown in the illustration, the monitor is OK; the problem will be with the PC's video system. Otherwise, you have a faulty monitor.

Hot tip

A monitor's test signal provides an easy and conclusive method of establishing if the monitor has failed completely.

Printers

If your printer refuses to print anything, your first move should be to switch it off and then back on. Doing so can resolve many configuration issues. If this doesn't work, do the same thing with the PC.

Next, establish whether the fault lies with the printer itself or with the system. This is done with the aid of the printer's test page facility; all printers have one of these.

The procedure varies from printer to printer, so you will have to consult the documentation. Typically, though, it involves isolating the device from the PC by disconnecting the interface cable, powering it up and then pressing a combination of buttons. If the printer is OK, it prints a page full of random characters. You then know that the problem is either a connection issue or is software related.

Assuming the printer itself is ok, the next thing to check is that the interface cable is securely connected. If it's a USB cable, try connecting it to a different USB port.

Then make sure the printer is correctly installed. Do this by opening Devices and Printers (Printers if you are running Windows Vista) in the Control Panel. If the device is installed it will be listed here. If it isn't, dig out the driver disk and reinstall it. While you have this window open, make sure that you don't have two or more copies of the driver installed. If you do, delete all of them and then install a single copy.

If you have more than one printer installed, make sure that the one malfunctioning is set as the default printer (click the device and from the Printer menu, select "Set as default printer" if it isn't).

Finally, check the application that you are printing from, as it is possible for a corrupt program to refuse to communicate with the printer. Type a few lines into Notepad and see if it prints.

If the test page doesn't print, check that the ink cartridges actually contain ink. Then run the head cleaning utility to make sure that the ink nozzles aren't simply blocked with dried ink. This is quite likely if the printer hasn't been used for a while.

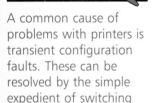

Hot tip

A common cause of problems with printers is transient configuration faults. These can be resolved by the simple expedient of switching off for a few seconds.

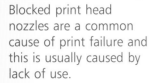

Hot tip

Blocked print head nozzles are a common cause of print failure and this is usually caused by lack of use.

Scanners

If nothing happens at all when you attempt to use the scanner, it will probably be because the system hasn't recognized it, i.e. it hasn't been installed correctly. You can check this in the Device Manager – the device should be listed in the Imaging Devices category but almost certainly won't be.

If it isn't, check the connections and reinstall the driver – this should resolve the issue. Also, if it's a USB model, don't forget to check that USB has been enabled in the BIOS.

If the system has recognized the scanner but it still doesn't work, you should be getting a "Scanner Initialization Failed", or similar, error message. The usual cause of this is that the device can't find the correct driver. This can be corrected in the scanner's software where you will find an option that enables you to select the driver the device is designed to use.

Another problem that can occur with USB powered scanners is the device drawing more power than the USB interface can deliver. This may trigger a "USB hub power exceeded" error message. The usual cause is having other USB powered devices connected to the system.

The temporary solution is to simply disconnect as many of the other devices as is necessary to make more power available to the scanner. For a permanent fix, you will need to buy an AC powered USB hub (shown right) that will supply all the power your USB devices need.

If you are already using a USB hub and the scanner suddenly stops working, try bypassing the hub by connecting the scanner directly to the PC. If it now works, the hub is faulty.

Problems can also be caused by the software being used in conjunction with the scanner. Most imaging programs, such as Adobe Photoshop, provide an option to import directly from a scanner, i.e. without using the scanning software supplied with the device. Eliminate this possibility by simply trying again with a different program.

Hot tip

A common problem with some scanners is initialization failure. If you get an error message to this effect, try rebooting the computer while the scanner is switched on. This action initializes the scanner's internal settings, and on restart, it will often work.

Optical Drives

Usually, when these devices have a physical problem, the relevant drive icon will be missing in My Computer.

Hot tip

Drive configuration issues relate to the communication channels assigned by Windows that enable the drive to communicate with the CPU. These problems can usually be resolved with the Device Manager.

Reboot the PC, and you should see the device listed on the first boot screen. If it isn't, the drive is either faulty or has a connection problem (if it's a newly installed drive, it will almost certainly be the latter). Open the system case and check that the power and interface cables are securely connected.

If the drive is listed on the boot screen but not in My Computer then it has a configuration problem (see margin note). See if the drive is listed in the Device Manager's "DVD/CD-ROM drives" category and whether any problems are reported there. If so, try the suggested remedy. Failing that, do the following:

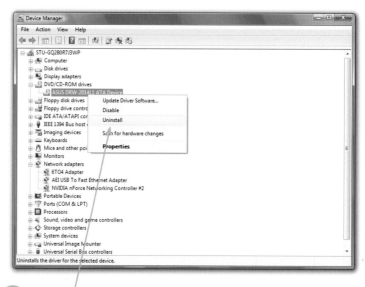

1 Right-click the drive and click Uninstall

2 Switch the computer off and physically disconnect the drive by removing both the power and interface cables. Then reconnect them and reboot. Windows will see the device as a new addition to the system and automatically assign it a new channel, which should resolve the issue

If the drive isn't listed in Device Manager, follow the procedure described in Step 2 above.

Repairing Windows

Windows Vista and Windows 7 offer users more tools with which to repair a faulty installation than previous versions have. These tools are located on the installation disk and so to use them, the PC must be set to boot from the CD/DVD drive as explained on page 86.

Then boot the PC from the installation disk and when you see the message "Press any key to boot from CD...", do so.

At the first screen, click Next and at the following screen, click Repair your computer. When the files have loaded, you will see the System Recovery Options screen as shown below:

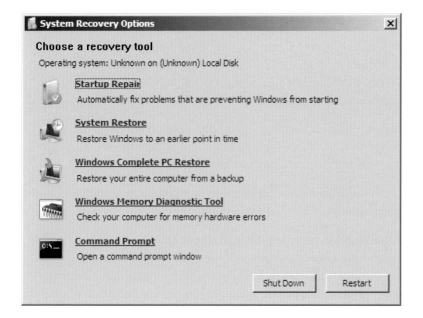

Startup Repair
The first option on the list, Startup Repair, is the one to choose if you are unable to start your PC. This will check the Windows startup files, which are the most likely cause of the problem, and if they are damaged it will replace them from the installation disk. The PC will then automatically reboot and all should now be well.

System Restore
If the PC still won't start however, the second option, System Restore, provides you with another line of attack.

...cont'd

System Restore is a utility that regularly creates and saves snapshots (known as Restore Points) on your computer. These restore points contain information about registry settings and other system information used by Windows.

When selected, System Restore will revert your system's settings to those in the chosen restore point. In other words, the system is "rolled back" to a working configuration.

Windows Complete PC Restore

If neither Startup Repair or System Restore can get the system going then you are running out of options. One possibility, before having to go the lengths of reinstalling Windows, is restoring the system from an image backup.

Don't forget

Before you can use the Windows Complete PC Restore utility, you must first make a backup of your system with the Backup and Restore utility. You will find this in the Control Panel.

This can be done by selecting the third System Recovery option, Windows Complete PC Restore, which replaces the current Windows installation with one from a previously made "mirror image" of the system.

Before you can do this though, you need to have created an image of your system via the Backup and Restore utility, which you will find in the Control Panel.

However, if you have neglected to create an image then you have no alternative but to reinstall Windows.

Windows Memory Diagnostic Tool

This utility checks the system's memory for errors and will usually run automatically when Windows detects a possible memory fault. However, it can be run manually, either from the Windows installation disk or from within Windows. To do the latter, go to Start, Control Panel, Administrative Tools, Windows Memory Diagnostic.

Command Prompt

Command Prompt is a text based utility that enables the user to perform many tasks on the PC. These include managing files, formatting and repartitioning hard drives, configuring how Windows boots, deleting and copying files, scanning the PC for viruses, as well as many other tasks.

Hot tip

For more information on the Command Prompt utility, press the F1 key and type Command Prompt into the Search box.

However, it is not a straightforward application and requires some knowledge to use it.

Index

O

P